EDUCATIONAL ADMINISTRATION GLOSSARY

EDUCATIONAL ADMINISTRATION GLOSSARY

Edward L. Dejnozka

GREENWOOD PRESS
Westport, Connecticut • London, England

Library of Congress Cataloging in Publication Data

Dejnozka, Edward L.
  Educational administration glossary.

  Bibliography: p.
  Includes index.
  1. School management and organization—Dictionaries.
I. Title.
LB15.D373   1984   371.2′003′21   83-5719
ISBN 0-313-23301-2 (lib. bdg.)

Copyright © 1983 by Edward L. Dejnozka

All rights reserved. No portion of this book may be reproduced, by any process or technique, without the express written consent of the publisher.

Library of Congress Catalog Card Number: 83-5719
ISBN: 0-313-23301-2

First published in 1983

Greenwood Press
A division of Congressional Information Service, Inc.
88 Post Road West, Westport, Connecticut 06881

Printed in the United States of America

10 9 8 7 6 5 4 3 2 1

Dedicated to:
Dean, Jeanne, Bruce, and Janice

CONTENTS

Preface	ix
Acknowledgments	xi
Glossary	1
Bibliography	179
Appendix I Statement of Ethics for School Administrators	195
Appendix II National and Regional Organizations of Interest to Educational Administrators	197
Appendix III Directory of State School Boards Associations	200
Appendix IV State Offices of the National PTA	205
Appendix V State Departments of Education	210
Appendix VI Regional Accrediting Associations	215
Appendix VII ERIC Clearinghouses	217
Appendix VIII Periodicals of General Interest to Educational Administrators	219
Appendix IX Journals Reviewed for Abstracting by *Educational Administration Abstracts*	222
Appendix X University Council for Educational Administration: Member Universities	225
Appendix XI University Council for Educational Administration: Partnership School Districts	226
Appendix XII U.S. Department of Education: Regional Offices	227

Contents

Appendix XIII Bureau of Indian Affairs: Area Offices	229
Appendix XIV NCATE-Accredited Programs: School Principalships, Supervision/Curriculum Development, and School Superintendency, 1982–1983	233
Appendix XV Key Governmental and Intergovernmental Offices	246

PREFACE

The field of educational administration is slightly more than a half-century old. Not unlike other professional occupations, it has, over the years, developed its own set of sub-specialties such as finance, law, supervision, and the like. And each of these, in turn, has developed its own terminologies—some new, some appropriated or adapted from cognate fields.

My purpose in preparing *Educational Administration Glossary* has been to identify these various terminologies, to define them, and to bring them together in the form of a single reference work. Such a resource, it is hoped, will prove useful to students, practitioners, and teachers of educational administration as well as others who might have need for a work of this type.

In time, of course, the nature and content of educational administration will change. Emerging and yet-to-be developed sub-specialties assuredly will produce new terminologies and thus require a more expansive volume of this type. My own efforts will be rewarded if the future scholars who will be preparing the more expansive versions will find this glossary to be a useful springboard for their work.

Preparation of *Educational Administration Glossary* entailed four basic and interrelated operations. Initially, a large number of books and periodicals dealing with educational administration were examined for the purpose of identifying candidate terms. In most instances, the terms identified appeared in more than one source and had some special kinship to educational administration. These selected terms were then placed on separate cards with accompanying notations made to indicate how each had been used and/or defined by others.

The second step, procedurally similar to the first, involved review and study of several supplementary sources such as government documents, books in cognate fields (e.g., personnel administration, management, accounting) and, on occasion, out-of-field glossaries.

The third step, preparation of a first-draft manuscript, involved the drafting of my own definitions. These, it should be noted, are presented in the context of education. In many cases, where a term may have noneducational as well as educational meaning, the former have generally been excluded.

Finally, a panel of reviewers was invited to validate my definitions and to suggest other terms that may have eluded me. The reviewers, identified in this volume's Acknowledgements section, represented different educational administration specialties. They were asked to critique each definition using three criteria, each posed as a question:

1. Is the term appropriate to the field of educational administration?
2. Is the definition correct (i.e., factually accurate and complete)?
3. Is the definition understandable?

Reviewers' written critiques were then studied and, in most instances, accommodated.

A number of Appendix items were then prepared. These supplement the Glossary section and, hopefully, increase this volume's resource value to its readers. Although every effort was made to insure the accuracy of each Appendix item at the time of publication, the reader is reminded that some of the information contained is dated, hence subject to some change from one year to the next.

ACKNOWLEDGMENTS

The author is indebted to a number of individuals for their assistance with this work.

As noted in the Preface, several colleagues, each conversant with one or more educational administration specialties, kindly agreed to critique my definitions and to suggest terms not included in the original manuscript. The critic readers were: Professor Zarif Bacilious, Chairman, Division of Administrative and Instructional Leadership, St. John's University; Dr. Anne Campbell, Commissioner of Education, Nebraska Department of Education; Richard M. Garten, Headmaster, Gulf Stream School, Florida; Professor Samuel Goldman, Dean, College of Human Resources, Southern Illinois University—Carbondale; Professor Harry J. Hartley, Department of Educational Administration, University of Connecticut; and, Professor W. Deane Wiley, Department of Educational Administration and Supervision, Southern Illinois University—Edwardsville.

Assistance of a different nature was received from another group of scholars, the 300 or so authors whose original works were studied in preparation for this volume and without whose writings this work could not have been completed. These authors and their works are listed in the Bibliography.

In addition, several individuals provided information or otherwise facilitated preparation of items appearing in the Appendix. They are: Dr. Lyn Gubser, Director, National Council for Accreditation of Teacher Education; Dr. Paul B. Salmon, Executive Director, American Association of School Administrators; Dr. Thomas A. Shannon, Executive Director, National School Boards Association; Dr. Ronald L. Smith, Executive Director, The National PTA; and, Dr. Charles L. Willis, Executive Director, University Council for Educational Administration.

Cynthia Harris, reference editor at Greenwood Press, offered numerous and helpful suggestions. Margaret (Peggy) Stone, reference librarian at Florida Atlantic University, was generous with time and technical assistance. Barbara Ludt, working from my handwritten 3x5 cards, meticulously prepared both the preliminary and final manuscript drafts.

Finally, I wish to express sincere appreciation to my wife, Mary (May) Dejnozka, for her clerical help, for her proofreading assistance, for her moral support during those periods when "things moved slowly," and for tolerating my absence during those many evening and week-end hours when I would withdraw to the study to play lexicographer.

GLOSSARY

A

AASA See *American Association of School Administrators.*

abatement Reduction of an already recorded expenditure; the amount deducted from the usual price for refunds, collections for loss/damage, discounts, and like reasons. Abatements usually apply to tax levies, special assessments, and service charges.

ability grouping The organization of student groups such that pupils in the same grade or subject are assigned to common classrooms, sections, or groups on the basis of reasonably similar learning ability. Such classification may result in the creation of two or more ability levels. See *tracking.*

absence STUDENT: Failure of a student to attend school (half-day or more) when it is in session. Student absences are classified as: (1) excused, or (2) unexcused. STAFF: Failure to be present to perform regularly assigned duties. Staff absences are of two types: (1) personal, or (2) professional.

academic freedom Intellectual independence. A generic term covering several rights for teachers. These include: (1) freedom to teach (i.e., free inquiry for teacher and student); (2) freedom to study; (3) freedom to express one's personal beliefs outside the classroom; (4) due process; and, (5) freedom to use materials of one's own choosing.

academic learning time See *time-on-task.*

academic retention See *nonpromotion.*

Academy for School Executives See *National Academy for School Executives.*

access time In data processing, the time that elapses between the instant information is called for from a retrieval system and the instant it is delivered. Sometimes used to indicate the time one has been allotted for use of a computer system.

account In financial accounting, a separate descriptive heading under which are recorded financial transactions that are similar (i.e., they have purpose, object, source, or some other characteristic in common). There are two broad classifications of accounts: (1) proprietary accounts (for assets, liabilities, and fund balances), and (2) budgetary accounts.

accountability Responsibility for achieving agreed-upon objectives, or performing a service, within a specified period of time, using stipulated resources. The answerable party, sometimes referred to as the steward, is held to account for performance in the context of predetermined objectives.

accounting system The recording, classifying, and reporting on the financial condition of a school, school system, or other governmental unit using appropriate financial statements, reports, and procedures.

accounts payable Unpaid balances owed to individuals, corporations, firms, or governmental units for goods and/or services received. Amounts due to other of the school system's funds are usually excluded.

accounts receivable Amounts owed to a school system by individuals, corporations, firms, or governmental units for goods and services provided by the system. Usually excluded are: (1) amounts due from other of the school system's funds, and (2) taxes receivable.

accreditation Official recognition by a state, regional, national agency/association attesting that the policies, procedures, and practices of a school, school system, or other institution meet the standards established by the reviewing agency/association. Accreditation is usually granted for a specified time period.

accrediting agency/association State, regional, or national organization, or private agency authorized to: (1) formulate evaluative criteria (standards); (2) judge educational institutions using these criteria; and (3) report findings and recommendations. Examples of such organizations are: (1) (regional) North Central Association of Schools and Colleges, (2) (national) National Council for Accreditation of Teacher

Education, (3) (state) individual state departments of education, and (4) (independent) independent school associations.

accrual basis A basis of accounting which records all revenues when earned and all costs when incurred. Revenues and costs are noted whether or not they have been paid.

accrued expenses Expenses which have been incurred and recorded but have yet to be paid.

accrued interest Interest that has accumulated but is not yet due.

accrued liability Monies that are owed but not yet due.

accrued revenue Taxes or other monies that have been earned but are not yet due.

achieved status Status that is earned and reflects considerable effort on the part of the individual. Examples: doctor, U.S. President, principal.

achievement test Examination that attempts to ascertain the mastery or acquisition level of a student's skills/knowledge in one or more subjects (e.g., reading, arithmetic) using certain (usually absolute) standards.

action research Term coined by Stephen M. Corey to describe local experimentation that does not employ the strict controls and demand the same rigor usually required of researchers. Such experimentation is often carried out to improve (change) curriculum or instructional practices.

activities program See *student activities program*.

activity funds Special funds established to record income/expenses related to student activities such as football games, concerts, and plays. All are considered school funds, hence subject to audit.

ad hoc committee A temporary committee charged with carrying out a specific, non-repetitive assignment. The committee is normally dissolved once its assignment has been completed.

ad valorem tax A tax or duty levied in proportion to the cost or value of the property being taxed. A fixed percentage (assessed value) of the item's true value is usually used for levy purposes. Examples of ad valorem taxes are property taxes, sales taxes, and a number of import duties.

adaptability The ability of institutions and leaders to adjust to change and/or to introduce new procedures/practices.

address Name, number, or code used in data processing to designate a particular location in storage. Sometimes referred to as the *operand* of an instruction.

adhocracy An approach to organizational management in which specialists or interested parties, regardless of their status within or outside the organization, are brought together to carry out a particular task or to help solve a specific problem. Such groups are disbanded once their assignments have been completed.

administration The process of directing and controlling the activities of a formal organization's members for the purpose of accomplishing institutional goals and objectives.

administration building Office building used to house a school system's central administration and its support staff.

administration internship See *internship*.

administrative assistant Or "assistant to," one who assists an executive officer, functioning in a staff rather than a line capacity.

administrative code Rules and regulations governing the operation of schools in a particular state. Such codes are normally formulated and/or enacted by state boards of education or chief state school officers (i.e., commissioners of education or state superintendents).

administrative law The rules and regulations created by agencies (e.g., school districts) legally authorized to regulate public activities. Such rules and regulations are subordinate to, and must be compatible with, applicable court decisions, legislation, and constitutions.

administrative remedy Action taken, or to be taken, by management to right some wrong or to resolve a problem; a step in the appeals process frequently required by law before an aggrieved party may seek assistance from the courts.

administrative skills Three basic administrative skills, identified by Robert L. Katz: (1) conceptual skills; (2) human skills; and (3) technical skills. Each, he contended, is related to the other two; further, the triad is seen as the basis for effective administration. See *conceptual skill, human skill,* and *technical skill.*

administrative tasks Activities for which the administrator is responsible. According to Paul F. Lazersfeld, there are four tasks common to all administrators: (1) fulfilling organizational goals; (2) using people, creatively and constructively, to help with goal realization; (3) establishing a wholesome and humane working climate for organizational members; and (4) providing for institutional innovation.

administrative team An organizational subsystem consisting of a school system's superintendent, other central office administrators, and building administrators. These administrative teams are created for the purposes of discussing administrative problems and/or integrating, reviewing, and refining members' roles and tasks. In the process, group decision-making activities are increased.

administrative unit Or basic unit of local school administration, a geographical area which, for educational purposes, is under the control of a single board of education.

administrator The individual responsible for directing and controlling the activities of an organization.

adult basic education Educational program that provides instruction in the basics to adults who never attended school or whose schooling was interrupted.

adult education Organized instructional program for mature learners who choose to pursue such instruction on a part-time basis. Participants are normally beyond the age of compulsory school attendance. Adult education includes but is not limited to offerings sponsored by a school system.

advanced placement Program, known formally as the Advanced Placement Program, that makes it possible for high school graduates to be examined in a subject-matter area (e.g., American history, English composition, chemistry, French). In areas where tests have been passed, college students are excused from taking the usual introductory course(s) and are assigned to more advanced course(s) instead. The examination is published by Educational Testing Service.

advertising sale Published notice of a school district's intent to sell bonds, a procedure required by state law.

advisory council A group of individuals who, by virtue of interest, expertise, or politics, offer advice or counsel to an administrator or to a governing board. Members may be elected or appointed to serve on a permanent or ad hoc basis (sometimes staggered). In education, advisory councils frequently include teachers and parents.

affected class In the context of affirmative action, individuals who continue to suffer the effects of discrimination (e.g., women, blacks). Such people are entitled to relief through use of an affirmative action plan. See *affirmative action*.

affective domain One of three behavior domains included in a taxonomy developed by Benjamin Bloom, et al. (1956). Behaviors assigned to this domain are those that pertain to emotions, feelings, and attitudes. See *cognitive domain* and *psychomotor domain*.

affirmative action Personnel program designed to insure equal employment opportunity, an outgrowth of the 1964 Civil Rights Act and subsequent legislation. Seeks, through the establishment of goals, to correct inequities that previously resulted in recruitment, employment, and upgrading of few or no minority and female applicants. Requires deliberate recruitment of qualified minority/female candidates and the institution of due process provisions for grievants.

affirmative action officer The individual designated to manage an organization's affirmative action plan and to see to its implementation by all units.

AFT See *American Federation of Teachers*.

age certificate An official document/statement certifying an individual's date of birth.

age-grade distribution Data (usually reported in table form) indicating the number or percentage of students in each grade, by age.

agency fee Or "fair share," a fee charged teachers or others who are not members of the employee organization authorized to bargain for them. The fee may be equal to the dues collected from unit members. The levying of such fees is legal in those states (approximately one-third) where special legislation permits this practice.

agency shop Provision in some collective bargaining agreements that requires all nonmembers of a recognized union to pay a monthly fee to the union. Such fees cover each nonmember's pro rata share of bargaining services rendered by the union.

aggregate days attendance The total of days present reported for all students during a specific reporting period.

aggregate days membership The total of days present and absent reported for all students during a specific reporting period.

agreement See *collective bargaining agreement*.

alien student A non-citizen permitted to enter the United States for the purpose of study.

aloofness One of four *principal behavior* dimensions included as a subtest in the OCDQ. The term is applied to principals who exhibit formal and impersonal ("by-the-book") behavior. See *Organizational Climate Description Questionnaire (OCDQ)*.

alphanumeric codes Computer codes that make use of letters, numbers, and other symbols such as punctuation. Also called "alphameric."

alternate bid Proposal, submitted by a bidding vendor/contractor, for materials, methods, or types of work that differ from what has been specified. Alternate bids, also known as "substitutions," may be requested by the school district or submitted voluntarily by a bidder.

alternative school A nonconventional school that students frequently attend voluntarily in place of conventional schools. It is usually a small, flexible school, public or independent, whose curriculum seeks to meet the unique needs of those enrolled; close teacher-pupil interaction and an "open" environment are common. Examples include: (1) schools for pregnant girls, gifted learners, disruptive students; (2) schools-without-walls; and (3) performing arts schools. See *magnet school*.

ambivalents One of three classes of employees who exhibit certain common behaviors relating to ambition. According to Robert Presthus, creator of the term, ambivalents: (1) constitute a small, disturbed percentage of all employees; (2) find it difficult to renounce their claims for status and power; (3) are unable to "play the disciplined role that would enable them to cash in such claims" (Presthus, p. 15); and (4) tend to be critical of the system in which they work. See *indifferents* and *upward mobiles.*

American Association of School Administrators (AASA) Primarily a school superintendents' organization; created in 1865 as the National Association of School Superintendents. AASA Publishes *The School Administrator,* a monthly newsletter.

American Education Week Annual observance honoring American schools and calling attention to education's needs; sponsored by the National Education Association, National Congress of Parents and Teachers, U.S. Department of Education, and the American Legion. The observance is conducted during the full week preceding Thanksgiving.

American Federation of Teachers (AFT) Nationwide union of teachers and other school employees. Established in 1916; currently affiliated with the American Federation of Labor-Congress of Industrial Organizations (AFL-CIO). AFT publishes *American Teacher,* a monthly newspaper, and *American Educator,* a quarterly journal.

androgogy Adult learning (as opposed to "pedagogy," which relates to learning by children).

anecdotal record An accumulation of written notes that describe what a child said or did in different situations. The record yields a behavior profile (i.e., pattern of interests, attitudes, difficulties) that can be helpful to counselors or other interventionists.

annual leave Leave time, with pay, accumulated during the year (e.g., two days for each month worked). Such leaves may be taken at any time, subject to employer approval; sick leave and other personnel benefits continue in force while the employee is on leave. Some school systems limit the number of accumulated leave days that can be carried forward from one school year to another.

annual report Yearly report, usually required, that describes an organization's (or unit's) achievements and, in some instances, its financial status.

annuity A series of money payments (equal amounts) made on a regular basis. These extend over a specific period of time. In education, common annuities include: (1) payments to retired personnel, and (2) payments made on term bonds.

anomie (1) In sociology, a condition characterized by the deterioration or general absence of norms or values in a group or society to guide individual and/or group behavior. (2) In psychology, feelings experienced by the individual who feels detached (i.e. alienated) from his society and its norms.

appeal procedure A formalized procedure that permits an employee, or an employee organization, to seek resolution of an impasse. Normally included are fact-finding and mediation provisions as well as a description of the hierarchical appeal channels.

applicant pool All applicants or those recruited in connection with a specific job vacancy and the group from which a selection is to be made.

applicant tally An affirmative action procedure in which the sex and minority status of all job applicants are recorded. Such information provides one basis for assessing the effectiveness of an organization's affirmative action plan.

apprenticeship Occupational experience a young person acquires through on-the-job training. Such training is normally carried out under the tutelage of a qualified practitioner.

appropriate education Special education term for an individualized program designed exclusively for an exceptional child. The program: (1) meets the child's unique needs; (2) covers a specified period of time; and (3) is cost-free to the child's parents.

appropriation Authorization granted by a legislative body (e.g., board of education) to make expenditures and to incur indebtedness for designated purposes. Such authorizations usually have time and dollar limits.

appropriation ledger A ledger in which are recorded all appropriations together with basic relevant information such as date and amount of original appropriation, transfers made into or out of each appropriation, encumbrances, and remaining balance.

aptitude test Examination that attempts to measure one's potential ability to do work or readiness to learn in a particular subject (e.g., music).

arbitration A method of settling employee-management disputes which involves use of a third party whose decision is usually final and binding. Arbitration is of three types: (1) *compulsory,* if required by law; (2) *advisory,* with decision(s) neither final nor binding; and (3) *voluntary,* with both parties volitionally agreeing to submit their dispute to arbitration. Arbitration is used frequently to interpret existing agreements, seldom to negotiate new ones.

arbitrator The impartial third party to whom disputing parties submit their differences for resolution; one empowered to make decisions (awards).

architectural barrier Obstacle, in or near a building, that makes the building or its components inaccessible to the physically handicapped.

area school A public school that offers specified instruction (e.g., vocational education) to residents of a particular geographic area. The area served is frequently larger than one school district.

area superintendent Administrator in a large school system who is responsible for all facets of school administration in one geographical part (area) of the district. He/she normally reports to the system's general superintendent.

area vocational school Regional, public vocational school serving senior high school students, post-secondary school students, and adults. Stimulated by the 1963 Vocational Education Act, area vocational schools offer occupational instruction other than professional. See *area school.*

argument See *hearing.*

articulation The coordination of programs and/or activities from level to level (e.g., middle school to high school) or area to area (e.g., department to department). See *horizontal articulation* and *vertical articulation.*

ASBO See *Association of School Business Officials of the United States and Canada.*

ASCD See *Association for Supervision and Curriculum Development.*

ascribed status In sociology, status that is inherited (e.g., royal title). See *achieved status.*

assault Threatening another with physical harm, thereby creating apprehension; a tort against one's mind. See *battery* and *tort*.

assessed value Economic value assigned to real estate or other property for tax-levying purposes. Such assignment is made by a governmental official known as an assessor. In many states, assessed value is lower than the property's market value.

assessed value, adjusted Mathematical adjustment (conversion) made to standardize the different actual assessment ratios used from one school district to another. Once such adjustment has been completed, meaningful district-to-district comparisons can be made.

assessed value per pupil The total assessed value of a school district divided by the district's average daily attendance (ADA) or average daily membership (ADM). See *average daily attendance* and *average daily membership*.

assessment center Process (not a place) in which a series of simulations and other realistic problems are presented to participants. Normally, 10–20 specific skills are evaluated to determine each participant's eligibility/suitability for a particular (frequently supervisory) position.

assessment ratio The assessed value of a property divided by its true (market) value.

assessment, special See *special assessment*.

assessments Techniques, instruments, and/or procedures used to evaluate students, teachers, or programs.

asset In education, property owned by a school system. A thing of value; may be monetary or nonmonetary, tangible or intangible.

assistant to See *administrative assistant*.

Association for Supervision and Curriculum Development (ASCD) A national professional organization made up of curriculum specialists, teachers, university professors, and school administrators/supervisors interested in supervision, curriculum, and teacher education. Organized in 1921, ASCD publishes *Educational Leadership,* a journal, eight times per year.

Association of School Business Officials of the United States and Canada (ASBO) International organization of noninstructional school leaders interested in school business administration. Formed in 1910; devoted to improvement of school business practices. ASBO publishes *School Business Affairs,* a monthly journal, and a newsletter.

assumption of risk A legal doctrine frequently used as a defense in tort actions. The doctrine holds that an individual who voluntarily exposes him/herself to a known property defect, and understands the potential danger associated with it, can not recover for injuries sustained. In schools, the doctrine has frequently been invoked in connection with athletic injuries.

assurance Synonym for insurance; primarily British usage.

attendance The physical presence of a student in a school or school system, or in a school sponsored activity (e.g., field trip) on a day when school is in regular session.

attendance area A geographic area served by a particular school.

attendance officer School official responsible for enforcing compulsory attendance laws. Investigates and analyzes cases of pupil non-attendance; formerly known as truant officer.

attendance register See *register of attendance.*

attendance unit A school or other organizational subdivision which has been designated to serve students residing in a particular geographical area.

attractive nuisance Legal concept which holds that individuals or institutions maintaining conditions, machinery, equipment, etc. on their premises, that are (1) potentially dangerous, and (2) likely to attract young children to such premises must take reasonable steps to protect children from such attractions.

audit A procedure for verifying the accuracy and checking on the security of an organization's accounting records. This procedure is completed periodically (e.g., annually) by an accountant or other independent third party. In addition to external audits, some organizations maintain an ongoing internal auditing system. Audits frequently include recommendations for improving accounting procedures. See *post-audit* and *pre-audit.*

authority Power granted by superiors for the purpose of carrying out responsibilities; the potential for getting things done in an organization, including the power to influence the actions of others.

authorization card Statement signed by an employee that: (1) authorizes an employee organization to act in his/her behalf, and (2) grants permission to an employer to withhold employee organization dues from the employee's pay. See *checkoff*.

autocratic leadership One of three commonly recognized types of leadership ("democratic" vs. "laissez-faire" vs. "autocratic") identified by Kurt Lewin and his colleagues (1939). The autocratic leader is one who is inclined to plan and to make decisions for the group; subordinates are treated dictatorially. See *democratic leadership* and *laissez-faire leadership*.

Automated Attendance Accounting System (AAA) A computerized system for checking student attendance. Small terminals, located in each classroom, are used by teachers to record individual student attendance.

autonomous climate One of six *organizational climates* identified through use of the OCDQ. Autonomous climate schools scored as follows on OCDQ subtests: (1) high "esprit"; (2) high "intimacy"; (3) low "disengagement"; (4) low "hindrance"; (5) high "aloofness"; (6) low "production emphasis"; (7) average "consideration"; and (8) average "thrust." See *Organizational Climate Description Questionnaire*.

auxiliary services Support services that serve as adjuncts to the instructional program. Among the most common are pupil transportation, food services, and health services.

average class size The total enrollment of all classes divided by the number of classes.

average daily attendance (ADA) The aggregate days' attendance of a school during a reporting period (e.g., term) divided by the number of days that school was in session.

average daily membership (ADM) The aggregate days' membership of a school (students officially enrolled) during a reporting period (e.g., term, month) divided by the number of days that school was in session.

award (1) In collective bargaining, the decision of an arbitrator. In most instances, it is binding on each of the disputing parties. (2) When used in the context of competitive bidding, the term refers to the identification of the successful bidder to whom a contract is to be offered. (3) Recognition (e.g. medal, certificate) for some outstanding achievement.

B

balance sheet A formal statement, properly classified, showing assets, liabilities, and fund reserves as of a particular date.

bank reconciliation statement A statement, normally completed at the end of each month and at the close of the year, reconciling the difference between a bank balance as shown in an institution's cash book and that shown on a current bank statement. Two factors generally account for the difference: (1) deposits not yet credited on the bank statement, and (2) outstanding checks not yet presented to the bank for payment.

bargaining unit Or negotiating unit (e.g., union), a group of employees recognized by an employer, or officially designated to represent an employee organization for collective bargaining purposes.

baseline In research, the initial (beginning) observations made before an innovation/intervention is introduced; the level with which post-intervention observations are compared.

BASIC *B*eginners *A*ll-purpose *S*ymbolic *I*nstruction *C*ode, a computer language that is relatively easy to learn and to use.

basic education Commonly used term for what some consider to be the "essential" school subjects (e.g., reading, computation, writing, geography, history, science).

basic school unit A school district that operates one or more schools and is governed by a single board of education; usually referred to as a school system.

batch Collections of papers, records, or programs that, for data processing purposes, are treated as a single unit.

batch processing In data processing the coding and grouping of items before they are processed.

battery (1) In law, the unpermitted act of making physical contact with another for the purpose of inflicting harm. A tort against one's person. (2) In measurement, a group of tests that have been standardized using a common population. Most frequently used are those that yield achievement scores in, and provide norms for, subtests in different curricular areas. See *assault* and *tort*.

bearer bond See *registered bond*.

behavior modification Techniques for shaping positive human behavior by employing learning principles associated with classical or operant conditioning (reinforcers). This approach is primarily identified with the work of B.F. Skinner.

behavioral objective Statement indicating what the postinstructional behavior of the learner should be. Generally, the behavioral objective is written and indicates: (1) what the learner should be able to do (i.e., performance) upon completion of instruction, and (2) the manner in which the intended behavior is to be evaluated.

bid An offer to provide materials or to render service at a particular price. These usually competitive offers are normally submitted in accordance with written specifications prepared by the school system seeking such materials/services.

bid bond A surety, submitted by a bidder on a school construction project, which accompanies the formal bid. The surety (usually a certified check or a surety-corporation bond) guarantees that the bidder, if chosen, will enter into a contract to complete the project at the sum specified in the bid.

bilingual education In American education, the use of two languages (one of which is English) as instructional vehicles for the same pupil population. Bilingual education programs are: (1) well organized; (2) cover all or part of the curriculum; and (3) include study of the history/culture associated with the mother tongue.

binary A condition/situation having but two possibilities. The binary number system, because of its base of 2 (compared to the base of 10 in the decimal system), is used in computers. The system's two digits are zero (0) and one (1).

bit Smallest unit of information recognized by a computer. Abbreviation of " *bi*nary digi*t*"; 0 or 1. See *binary*.

blanket insurance Insurance covering more than one item of property at a single location or several property items at more than one location.

block grant A type of grant, distributed (usually by the federal and state government) by means of a formula, that became popular in the 1960's and 1970's. Unlike categorical grants, which earmark funds for specific purposes, block grants provide recipients with considerable latitude to spend awarded funds as they best see fit.

board of education, local An appointed or elected body possessing legal power to govern a local school district. The board of a public school system is an agency of government created by the state legislature. Its principal functions are policy-making, appraising, legislating, financing, and authorizing. Such bodies are sometimes referred to as school boards, boards of trustees, boards of directors, school trustees, or school committees. Some governing bodies of nonpublic schools/systems are also known as boards of education.

board of education, state The body, legally constituted, responsible for the general supervision of elementary and secondary education in a particular state. Some state boards of education also have varying degrees of responsibility for overseeing higher education.

board secretary The individual officially designated to serve the board of education in a secretarial capacity. Functions associated with this position are essentially clerical in nature (e.g., keeping of minutes). In some states, the position is referred to as "clerk of the board."

boarding school See *residential school*.

body, corporate See *corporate body*.

body language Information communicated through movements of the body, facial expressions, or voice inflection. Such communication may be intentional or unintentional.

bond An instrument of indebtedness; a written promise to pay a specific sum of money (face value) at some fixed future time (maturity date) and carrying a fixed rate of interest (usually payable in regular installments). See *callable bonds, general obligation bonds* and *serial bonds.*

bond anticipation note Short-term, interest-bearing note issued by a school system in anticipation of soon-to-be-issued bonds. Notes are retired using proceeds from the related bond sale.

bond attorney The attorney who approves, and certifies as to the legality of a bond issue.

bond discount The difference between the face value of a bond and the actual amount paid for it (exclusive of accrued interest).

bond rating An estimate of a school district's, corporation's, or government's ability to repay bonds that it has issued. Bond rating firms such as Moody's and Dun and Bradstreet evaluate and rank the issuing agency's bonds on the basis of safety, this generally reflecting factors such as the agency's repayment history, management, and economic condition.

bond register Official and complete record of a school system's bonds. Data recorded include facts such as: (1) number of each bond issued/redeemed; (2) dates of issue and redemptions; and (3) principal and interest payments made.

bonded debt Or funded debt, the total dollar value of a school system's outstanding bonds.

breach of contract In law, the failure to perform a duty or to comply with conditions prescribed in a contract.

brief In law, a written summary of a case or a written statement, prepared by each side in a legal dispute, that highlights each side's position to the court.

British Infant School See *infant school.*

Buckley Amendment Federal legislation (1974) requiring that, subject to certain specific conditions, student files be open to parents or students over the age of 18. Additionally, provision is made for challenging materials in the file that are deemed to be inappropriate.

buddy system See *peer supervision*.

budget A financial plan, expressed in dollars and covering a period of time (usually one fiscal year). Budgets typically include: (1) a budget message (rationale and summary); (2) enumeration of anticipated expenditures; and (3) anticipated revenues. Information as to previous years' expenditures and revenues is frequently provided for purposes of comparison.

budget, line-item A budget format in which individual expenditures are listed as separate transactions. When most rigorously employed, single positions and equipment items (i.e. objects of expense) are listed as separate expenditures. See *budget, program*.

budget message A narrative statement that: (1) highlights the contents of the budget; (2) presents the philosophy, aims, and achievements that undergird its proposals; and (3) interprets the budget using brief explanations and/or graphics.

budget, program A management tool that attempts to relate costs with results. Program budgets are concerned with various services to be provided as opposed to object budgets that traditionally indicate what is to be bought. Program budgets are generally used for planning rather than accounting purposes. See *budget, line-item*.

budgetary account See *account*.

budgetary calendar A written chronology indicating the dates by which specific budgetary tasks are to be completed by the school business administrator and/or others involved in budget formulation.

bureaucracy Ideal model of an organizational system, described by German sociologist Max Weber, that includes the following components: (1) high specificity of goals; (2) a functional division of labor; (3) a specialized administrative structure; (4) rules describing employee rights and obligations; (5) selection of individuals on the basis of their technical competence; (6) procedures describing work to be performed; and (7) impersonal norms of conduct.

bureaucratization The opposite of debureaucratization. Defined by S.N. Eisenstadt as the extension of a bureaucracy's power and sphere of activities. New activities are assumed, or existing ones broadened, as the bureaucracy's influence over others is extended. See *bureacracy* and *debureaucratization*.

business administration See *school business administration.*

business manager In a school system, the individual responsible for managing the system's business administration functions (e.g., accounting, food services, pupil transportation, purchasing, buildings and grounds, etc.).

byte Generic data processing term for a grouping of adjacent binary digits that the computer can act upon as a unit (e.g., an 8-bit byte, a 6-bit byte). See *bit.*

C

cafetorium A large, open room in a school that can be used: (1) as a cafeteria, and (2) as an auditorium; a multi-purpose room.

callable bonds Or optional bonds, bonds that may be "called in" (redeemed) by the borrower (e.g., school district), at the borrower's option and with appropriate notice, prior to the stated maturity date. Many callable bonds prescribe a minimum number of years during which bonds cannot be called.

Cambridge Plan Plan for organizing a nine-year elementary school's curriculum, introduced (1893) by Superintendent Charles Cogswell (Cambridge, MA schools). Study material in grades 1–3 was common to all students. Two parallel tracks were created for grades 4–9—to be completed in six years by most students, in four years by brighter students. In 1910, a two-track, eight-year curriculum was substituted.

capacity See *normal capacity*.

capital budget A fiscal budget that projects capital outlays and indicates how these are to be financed. It is usually presented as a component of a school system's current budget. Sometimes referred to as a *capital program*. See *capital outlay*.

capital outlay Or capital expenditures, money spent for the acquisition of, addition to, or replacement of fixed assets—notably land, buildings, and new equipment. Such fixed assets are presumed to have more than a one-year life.

capital program See *capital budget*.

card deck Group of punch cards having some characteristic(s) in common.

card punch See *keypunch*.

Cardinal Principles of Secondary Education Widely publicized statement of objectives for the American high school, authored in 1918 by the National Education Association's Commission on Reorganization of Secondary Education. Seven basic objectives for the individual were cited: (1) health; (2) command of fundamental processes; (3) worthy home membership; (4) vocational competence; (5) citizenship; (6) worthy use of leisure; and (7) ethical character.

"career-bound" administrators Term coined by Richard O. Carlson to describe school superintendents who move readily from one school system to another to achieve professional advancement. Carlson distinguished these superintendents from a second type, the "place-bound" administrators. See *"place-bound" administrators*.

career education Activities that attempt to blend academic and occupational learning programs. Students, at all grade levels, learn about and prepare to participate in the world of work.

Carnegie unit Unit of academic credit used in secondary schools. One unit is normally earned by a student upon completion of a course involving at least 120 clock hours of class work. Sixteen units or more are normally required to qualify for a diploma.

carrel Semi-isolated booth in which students can study independently; usually located in school libraries and resource centers, sometimes in classrooms.

carrier Insurer, or insurance carrier; usually an insurance company.

CASA See *Committee for the Advancement of School Administration*.

case conference Technique for bringing together a group of professionals (e.g., principal, selected teachers, counselor) to discuss the problems of an individual student. Participants share information about the pupil and proceed to formulate a plan of action for helping him/her. Student problems frequently reflect adjustment difficulties.

case law Sometimes referred to as common law, law that has its basis in the cases previously decided by the courts, as distinguished from the law derived from statutes.

case load The number of students assigned to a professional staff member (e.g., counselor, psychologist) for the purpose of receiving a particular kind of educational service.

case method A method of carrying out social research (including management). Specific organizational or legal problems are examined; participants then offer solutions based on: (1) information made available in the case, and (2) their knowledge of the subject.

case study In-depth examination of one person, event, or organization, normally carried out over an extended period of time.

cash Currency, checks, coin, bank drafts, or money orders on hand or on deposit.

cash basis accounting An accounting system in which revenues are recorded when received; similarly, expenditures are recorded only when paid.

cash book A ledger in which only "cash" receipts and "cash" payments are recorded. Open and closing balances are reported at regular intervals of time (e.g., monthly).

cash discount Price allowance granted to a buyer for having made payment(s) at time of purchase or within a stipulated period of time.

cash flow The inflow and outflow of cash resulting from operations, borrowing, and the like; affected by receipts and expenditures.

categorical aid Or categorical grant, support funds from a higher governmental level that are earmarked for a specific purpose. School systems receive such aid from both the federal and state governments (e.g., Title I funds, vocational education aid). At the federal level, some categorical grants are distributed by formula, others as competitive project grants.

CCSSO See *Council of Chief State School Officers.*

census See *school census.*

census tracts Geographical subdivisions into which cities, other municipalities, school districts, and other governmental units are divided for the purpose of gathering demographic data. See *school census.*

central administration Personnel who direct the affairs of a total educational system as distinguished from those whose activities are limited to one school.

central kitchen Single kitchen in which all or most food is prepared and from which it is distributed to local (frequently small) schools; an alternative to individual school kitchens.

central tendency In statistics, the single most typical score for a group of scores; the score around which other scores tend to cluster. Measures of central tendency include the mean (average), median, and mode. See *mean, median,* and *mode.*

certificate A license, issued by a state, authorizing one to engage in some specific form of educational practice.

Certificate of High School Equivalency Frequently referred to as an equivalency diploma, a document issued to an individual who has not completed high school but has fulfilled requirements for high school graduation. One customarily qualifies for the Certificate by passing the Tests of General Educational Development (GED).

certificated personnel Individuals specifically trained and licensed (i.e., certified) to perform educational services.

certification (1) In education, the process of licensing individuals to engage in a specific form of educational practice (e.g., teacher, counselor). (2) When used in collective bargaining, refers to official recognition that an employee organization has been chosen by a majority of employees to serve as their bargaining representative. See *certificate* and *competency-based certification.*

certification reciprocity See *reciprocity.*

chain of command Or administrative chain of command, the formal control and communication channels in an organization through which instructions and information are passed. Instructions are passed downward; information flows upward, downward, or laterally.

change In a system, the alteration, modification, or discontinuance of a goal, structure, or process.

change agent Individual who works to produce change in an organization. The change agent is frequently, though not always, an outside professional who has little personal involvement with those in the system he/she seeks to change. Synonyms sometimes used for change agent are "interventionist" or "organization development consultant."

change order A written order, issued by an architect following consultation with his/her client, for one or more changes in the plans of a building during the course of its construction. Such orders may involve cost changes.

change, organizational See *organizational change*.

change strategy See *strategy*.

charismatic leadership A leadership style which reflects an individual's ability to lead others more because of personal magnetism than legal authority.

checklist A type of rating scale used to evaluate one's ability to perform specific performance standards. Those doing the evaluating check what they consider to be the appropriate assessment category for each standard (e.g., satisfactory, unsatisfactory; yes, no). See *descriptive scales* and *numerical scales*.

checkoff A practice whereby an employer, per agreement with an employee organization and subject to written authorization by each employee (as required by law/agreement), regularly withholds organizational dues from employees' salary payments and transmits these funds to the employee organization.

chief executive The individual who serves as administrative head of an organization and normally reports to a governing board.

chief school administrator Or chief school official; at the school district level, the superintendent of schools.

chief state school officer The chief executive officer of a state department of education. His/her title varies from one state to another. Commonly used titles are Commissioner of Education, State Superintendent of Instruction, and State Superintendent of Public Instruction.

child accounting See *student accounting*.

child advocate One who works to define, protect, and guarantee the rights of children.

child benefit theory Legal theory enunciated by the U.S. Supreme Court (*Cochran v. Louisiana State Board of Education*) which holds that public monies may be used to provide benefits (e.g., textbooks, busing) for nonpublic school children so long as such expenditures benefit the child and not the school.

child-find The process used by education officials and other agency representatives to identify and locate children who: (1) require special education services and are not receiving them, or (2) require an improved type of special education service.

chronological age One's actual age, expressed in years and months; time elapsed since one's birth.

city district Usually a large school district whose boundaries are coterminous with those of a city.

civil rights Rights, granted by the U.S. Constitution and derived from statutes, guaranteeing that citizens may not be discriminated against in areas such as voting, housing, or education because of their race, sex, religion, color, or national origin.

class standing Rank in class based on grade point average.

classified personnel Nonprofessional employees of a school or school system (e.g., secretaries, custodians, guards).

clerk-of-the-works Individual employed by an owner (e.g., board of education) to supervise construction projects on a full-time basis. Construction irregularities are reported to the architect for corrective action, and to the owner.

clerk, school board See *board secretary*.

climate, autonomous See *autonomous climate*.

climate, closed See *closed climate*.

climate, controlled See *controlled climate*.

climate, familiar See *familiar climate*.

climate, open See *open climate*.

climate, organizational See *organizational climate*.

clinical supervision A five-stage supervisory procedure, developed by Morris L. Cogan and his associates, that involves close interaction between a teacher and a supervisor and emphasizes improvement of the teacher's classroom performance. The five stages are: (1) preobservation conference; (2) observation; (3) analysis and strategy; (4) supervision conference; and (5) postconference analysis. Rapport and mutual commitment to goals are key elements.

clique Informal, usually small groups or associations of people in an organization who have common interests/sentiments. Members may or may not be of equal rank or work in the same units (i.e, department).

closed climate One of six *organizational climates* identified through use of the OCDQ. Closed climate schools scored as follows on OCDQ subtests: (1) high "disengagement"; (2) high "hindrance"; (3) average "intimacy"; (4) low "esprit"; (5) low "thrust"; (6) high "aloofness"; (7) high "production emphasis"; and (8) low "consideration." See *Organizational Climate Description Questionnaire*.

closed loop model A graphic illustrating a procedure for monitoring group performance. The model consists of several sequential steps, the principal ones being: (1) establishment of objectives; (2) establishment of performance standards; (3) development of an action plan; and (4) analysis of performance.

closed shop Condition of a collective bargaining agreement under which the employer may employ and retain only union members in good standing. The closed shop is illegal for industries engaged in interstate commerce. See *open shop* and *union shop*.

closed system An organizational system that neither recognizes nor accommodates external environmental factors or pressures. Unlike open systems, which do interact with their environments, closed systems make no such exchanges; their boundaries resist penetration.

COBOL Programming language used in business data processing. Acronym for *c*ommon *b*usiness *o*riented *l*anguage.

cocurricular activities Or extra-curricular activities, voluntary, school-sponsored activities that supplement the basic curriculum and for which academic credit is not granted. Examples: band, football, Spanish Club.

cocurricular funds See *activity funds*.

code (1) In data processing, a system of symbols (e.g., numbers, letters) used to represent specific items or categories of information. (2) In law, a collection of laws (e.g., school code).

code of behavior See *student code*.

code of ethics A written standard of acceptable behavior for members of a profession or government personnel. Some prescribe sanctions for code violators. No universal code has been developed for educational administrators; however, some organizations (e.g., National Association of Secondary School Principals) have formulated their own ethics statements.

code, school See *school code*.

code, student See *student code*.

coding A system of numbering or otherwise categorizing school board policies, business accounts and other financial information, library books, etc. Symbols used make it possible to obtain information readily. When used as a data processing term, coding refers to the writing of computer instructions and data.

coeducation Organizational system in which students of both sexes are enrolled in the same school or class.

coefficient of correlation A measure indicating the relationship, or "going-togetherness," of two variables (e.g., test scores) for a particular population. Product moment "r," the coefficient often used to report the nature and degree of such relationship, ranges from +1.00 (to indicate perfect positive correlation), to −1.00 (perfect negative correlation).

coercive power Power one enjoys in an organization that is based on his/her ability to punish other organizational members (e.g., deny favors, salary increases, promotions). One of five forms of power identified by John R.P. French, Jr. and Bertram Raven. See *expert power, legitimate power, referent power,* and *reward power*; also see *compliance typology*.

cognition General term for the process by which knowledge is acquired; actual "knowing" (the product of such process).

cognitive domain One of three behavior domains included in a taxonomy developed by Benjamin Bloom, et al. (1956). Behaviors listed in this domain are those that deal with the mental process of recall, reasoning, comprehension, and judgment. See *affective domain* and *psychomotor domain*.

cohesiveness The attractiveness a group has for its members. Factors contributing to cohesiveness include group size, the status of the group, members' agreement regarding group goals, and interpersonal relationship. The group remains attractive to the extent that individual needs are being met.

cohort survival method A technique for predicting future student enrollments. Average survival ratios are established for each grade level (i.e., percentage of last year's fourth graders who are in this year's fifth grade) and then multiplied by the latest grade enrollment figures available.

coinsurance Type of insurance that requires the policyholder to purchase a specified percentage (e.g., 80%) of coverage based on the real value of the insured property. In case of loss, both the insurer and the insured contribute on a pro-rata basis. Such arrangements result in lower premiums.

COLA Acronym for *c*ost *o*f *l*iving *a*djustment. See *cost-of-living adjustment*.

Coleman Report Popular designation of a widely-circulated study by James Coleman, completed under U.S. government auspices. The study examined factors relating to students' academic achievement. A major (and controversial) finding was that peers and family are more significant as conditioners of achievement than is the school.

collateral benefit Fringe benefit; employee benefit that supplements basic compensation.

collective bargaining The process whereby salaries and other conditions of employment are determined by representatives of the employees and the employer through direct negotiations. Thereafter, a written document (contract, or agreement) is executed that incorporates all mutually acceptable agreements reached.

collective bargaining agreement Written contract which includes the terms of a settlement agreed to by an employer and employee representatives. Agreements normally include: (1) the period of time covered; (2) specific conditions of employment such as wages, fringe benefits, holidays, etc.; and (3) procedures to be followed to resolve disputes arising during the term of the contract.

collective negotiations A semantic compromise, attributed to Myron Lieberman, that fuses "collective bargaining," a union term, with "professional negotiations," the counterpart term used by the National Education Association.

Commerce Business Daily A U.S. Department of Commerce publication, published every weekday, in which all federal procurement invitations are listed. Listings include U.S. Education Department requests for proposals/contracts.

Committee for the Advancement of School Administration (CASA) Committee established by the American Association of School Administrators (1955) with a grant from the W.K. Kellogg Foundation. Major activities/recommendations related to: (1) raising certification requirements for administrators; (2) making accreditation standards more rigorous for administrator preparation programs; and (3) improving dissemination of research findings.

common law See *case law*.

common school district Type of school district organization found in some eastern, central, and most western states. These administrative units tend to be small, rural, and have boundaries that are not coterminous with those of any other governmental units. Numbers of common school districts have disappeared in recent years through consolidation with other school systems.

common schools The earliest public schools operated in the U.S. They were: (1) open to all children; (2) had no admission requirements; and (3) generally accommodated students who did not attend Latin grammar schools. The common school movement was established in the early 1800's.

communication The process through which one individual exchanges information, opinions, and feelings with others; media used may be speech, behavior, or writing. In organizations, a two-way process that involves transmission of information/decisions from one member to another. Communication takes place once the message transmitted is received. See *formal communication* and *informal communication*.

community analysis Study (survey) of a school community for purposes such as identification of educational needs or ascertaining community expectations of the schools. May be undertaken in conjunction with the development of a new program or budget, or simply as a basis for establishing an effective school-community relations program.

community control In large cities, the allocation of power to local communities with the expectation that they will have increased governing authority over their schools.

community council In education, a group of local residents who provide general counsel and/or specialized assistance to the schools. Community councils are used extensively in the field of community education, serving a liaison role linking community with the local community school director.

community education Concept recognizing that all community residents, regardless of age or educational background, have educational needs that should be provided by the school. Educational programming is based on the philosophy of lifelong learning.

community relations See *school-community relations*.

community school Educational institution (elementary, secondary, or adult), operated by a local board of education, whose programs meet the learning needs of all or most people in the community. Normally includes a regular day program for students of mandatory school age as well as an optional program (day or night) featuring diverse activities that reflect the needs and interests of all or most residents.

community school coordinator Professional responsible for coordinating the several community school directors working in a school district. See *community school director*.

community school director Professional responsible for administering community education in a local community school. He/she reports to the building principal and plays a liaison role between school and community. See *community school coordinator*.

community services Services provided by the school for the benefit of community residents, exclusive of public school and adult education programs. Included are activities such as recreation, community welfare, civic affairs, and public libraries.

comparative negligence Legal doctrine that determines (compares) the degree of negligence attributable to both plaintiff and defendant in cases where the opposing parties have each contributed to an injury. In some states, the classifications "slight," "ordinary," or "gross" are used; in others, juries determine the negligence ratio for each party. This doctrine replaces contributory negligence in some states. See *contributory negligence*.

compensatory damages See *damages*.

compensatory education Special programs designed to serve the special educational needs of children who, for social and/or economic reasons, are educationally impoverished. Many such programs were initiated in the 1960's in conjunction with the school desegregation movement with considerable emphasis placed on reading and language arts instruction.

competence Demonstrated ability to perform satisfactorily. Refers to actual patterns of behavior observed in an individual; not to be confused with competencies. See *competencies*.

competencies Descriptions of expected, needed, or yet-to-be demonstrated performance; the specification of anticipated behaviors, skills, knowledge, or attitudes, usually set forth as conditions for role fulfillment or as learning tasks to be performed.

competency-based certification Process employed by a state or other authorized agency that requires applicants for a professional credential to demonstrate mastery of certain basic competencies. Mastery may be demonstrated through written examination or other prescribed procedures.

competency-based education (CBE) Curriculum or program of studies organized around a predetermined set of competencies (e.g., skills, knowledge, attitudes). Learning activities are planned to help the learner to master the prescribed competencies.

competitive bid See *bid*.

compliance Behavior exhibited by an employee which suggests that he/she is basically committed to the goals of the organization and is contributing to their realization. Various compliance strategies are employed by leaders to bring about such behavior. See *compliance typology*.

compliance typology A classification, formulated by Amitai Etzioni, consisting of three means by which leaders can get subordinates to comply with organizational objectives: (1) "coercive power," threatening physical type of punishment (e.g., suspension, corporal punishment); (2) "remunerative power," the doling out of monetary rewards; and (3) "normative power," the use of symbolic and value elements to induce compliance (e.g. status, praise).

comprehensive high school A general-purpose secondary school that provides a diversified program to meet the educational needs of its heterogeneous clientele. To meet students' varying abilities and interests, the school's curriculum includes academic, vocational, avocational, and general courses.

compulsory school attendance age The age span, established by law, during which a child is required to attend school (e.g., 7–16).

compulsory school attendance legislation State laws requiring children to attend school if they fall within the prescribed chronological age span (e.g., 7–16). The first such law was passed in Massachusetts (1852).

computer-assisted instruction (CAI) System of programmed learning that makes use of a computer; features instant feedback. CAI is normally carried out in a classroom and may include any or all of the following: inquiry, drill, problem-solving, simulation, statistical data, and graphics.

computer-managed instruction The use of a computer to record the progress of individual students as they advance through a learning sequence. Lessons are planned, tests scored, etc. for the benfit of both teacher and learner. (Not to be confused with computer-assisted instruction.)

concept six A year-round school plan that divides the year into six equal parts (i.e., two months each). Students attend school for four parts, vacation during the other two. They may elect to be present for five parts for enrichment or acceleration purposes.

conceptual skill One of three basic administrative skills (the others being "human skill" and "technical skill"). Conceptual skill is the ability to organize information cognitively and to apply such information to practice; the ability to see the organization as a whole and to understand the workings and interdependence of its several parts. See *human skill* and *technical skill*.

conciliation Occasionally used synonym for "mediation." See *mediation*.

condemnation The acquisition of private property for public use, subject to law, when the owner is reluctant to sell his/her property. In some states, school land can be condemned by other governmental agencies after need has been established. See *eminent domain*.

condemnation proceedings The process governmental units (including school districts) follow to acquire privately-owned property through the right of eminent domain. See *eminent domain*.

confirmation order A written purchase order prepared as follow-up to an order that has been placed verbally, usually via telephone. This procedure is generally discouraged by school business officials except in those cases where immediate orders must be placed.

conflict Also known as "group conflict" or "organizational conflict," opposition within an organization that grows out of diverse and incompatible views. Serious conflict heightens tension and causes opposing groups to work toward incompatible goals.

conflict matrix Chart used in departmentalized schools (usually high schools) that lists one-section classes which, if scheduled in the same class period, would result in conflicts. A widely-used procedure prior to the advent of computerized scheduling.

consideration (1) One of two leader behavior dimensions measured by the Leader Behavior Description Questionnaire (LBDQ). Factors comprising consideration are those related to concern for people (e.g., friendship, warm relationship with staff) and group maintenance. (The second LBDQ dimension is "initiating structure.") (2) One of four dimensions of principal behavior as measured by the Organizational Climate Description Questionnaire (OCDQ). As used in this latter instrument, consideration is characterized by the principal who treats teachers "humanly."

consolidation Or school district reorganization, the merging of two or more school districts for the purpose of phasing out those that are small and inefficient. Such reorganization is a state responsibility. As a result of consolidation, the number of U.S. school districts has been reduced from 94,926 in 1947–48 to approximately 16,000 in 1983.

consortium A group of independent organizations (e.g., universities) engaged in a single effort in which each has an interest and from which each presumably benefits.

constant dollars Dollar amounts that have been adjusted to eliminate inflationary factors. This adjustment makes possible meaningful year-to-year comparisons. To facilitate comparisons, a base year (e.g. 1974 = 1.00) is established.

construction fund Separate fund used to finance: (1) the construction of new school buildings; (2) additions to existing buildings; (3) land; and (4) related equipment.

consultant Resource person retained from outside the organization, sometimes chosen from within to: (1) provide advice, (2) perform some specific labor, or (3) assist in bringing about some type of change.

consumer price index (CPI) Monthly statistic prepared by the U.S. Bureau of Labor Statistics that compares current prices to those of some predetermined base year. The index is expressed as a percentage

$$\text{(i.e., CPI} = \frac{\text{current price}}{\text{base year price}} \times 100).$$

contingency management Or situational management, a flexible style of leadership that is based on sound management theory but which takes local (situational) factors/conditions into account. See *contingency theory* and *situational sensitivity*.

contingency theory Theory emphasizing that there is no one ideal organizational structure or leadership style. Rather, the appropriate pattern, or "fit," is contingent upon local circumstances and resources (e.g., the job to be done, kinds of employees, environmental factors, organizational goals).

contingent fund Monies set aside for payment of unanticipated expenditures or anticipated expenditures for which the amount is not known.

continuing contract A contract that is renewed annually and automatically, but which may be terminated for cause. In education, the term generally applies to automatic contract renewals for tenured personnel.

continuing education Instructional program for adults and youth who have passed the age of compulsory education.

continuous progress plan See *nongraded school plan* and *nongrading*.

continuous promotion Synonym for social promotion. Students are advanced from one grade level to the next on the basis of chronological age.

continuous service Employment uninterrupted by a break in service.

contract An agreement between two parties. Three factors are involved: (1) the contracting parties are legally eligible to participate; (2) some consideration (i.e., money or something of value that is promised); and (3) mutual agreement as to the meaning of the contract.

contract administration The process of implementing a contract with an employee organization that has been achieved through collective bargaining.

contracted services Services rendered to a school or school system by persons who are not on the payroll. For accounting purposes, all expenses related to the rendered service are included.

contributory See *noncontributory*.

contributory negligence Action, or failure to act (i.e., negligent behavior) by the complaining party (i.e., plaintiff) that contributed to the injury. In some states, if evidence shows that plaintiff acted in a negligent manner, there can be no recovery. See *comparative negligence*.

control Process by which organizational activities are monitored and regulated to insure that organizational objectives are being met.

controlled climate One of six *organizational climates* identified through use of the OCDQ. Controlled climate schools scored as follows on OCDQ subtests: (1) high "esprit"; (2) low "disengagement"; (3) high "production emphasis"; (4) low "consideration"; (5) high "thrust"; (6) average "aloofness"; (7) high "hindrance"; and (8) low "intimacy." See *Organizational Climate Description Questionnaire*.

conventional schedule Traditional (usually secondary school) student schedule made up of class periods that are uniform in length and generally do not vary from one day to the next. See *modular schedule*.

cooperating administrator The practicing educational administrator selected to assist, direct, and participate in the evaluation of an administrative intern's field work. See *internship*.

cooperating teacher Or critic teacher, the practicing teacher selected to supervise the day-to-day work of a student teacher. Cooperating teachers are normally chosen because of their experience and record of success in the classroom.

cooperative education Or cooperative vocational education, an organized educational program that correlates academic instruction with on-the-job training.

Cooperative Program in Educational Administration (CPEA) An early research and development program in educational administration; initiated in 1950 with W. K. Kellogg Foundation support. CPEA Project Centers were organized on eight university campuses to study administrative practice and programs for training school leaders.

cooperative vocational education See *cooperative education*.

cooptation Defined by Philip Selznick (*American Sociological Review*, February 1948, p. 34) as "the process of absorbing new elements into the leadership or policy-determining structure of an organization as a means of averting threats to its stability or existence"; an organizational defense mechanism. Sometimes involves the sharing of unit or organizational decision-making power.

coordination An element of the administrative process which ensures that the different parts of an organization are interrelating effectively; synchronizing and unifying institutional resources for the purpose of realizing organizational goals with a minimum of conflict, time, and effort.

core current expenditures All expenditures exclusive of transportation and food service costs. This measure is sometimes used for purposes of interstate comparison.

corporal punishment Infliction of physical punishment to the body of a student for the purpose of deterring future misconduct.

corporate body Or body corporate, a legally constituted agency authorized to carry out specified functions. A board of education, for example, is a corporate body. Its authority resides in the total board, not in any of its individual members.

corrective maintenance Ongoing repairs to a school or its equipment.

correlation coefficient See *coefficient of correlation*.

cosmopolitans A term coined by Alvin W. Gouldner to describe workers in an organization who are: (1) low on loyalty to their organizations; (2) high on commitment to their specialization or professional skills; and (3) likely to identify with an outside (as opposed to local) reference group. Gouldner identified two types of cosmopolitans: the "outsiders" and the "empire builders." See *locals*.

cost accounting An accounting system for classifying, recording, allocating, and analyzing the cost of a particular process, school, program, department, or product. The system serves at least three related functions: (1) providing cost histories; (2) projecting future costs; and (3) helping the administrator to make effective decisions.

cost benefit analysis An analytical technique for comparing the benefits expected to accrue with investments made. Basically, the technique serves to answer the question: What will be the total dollar or social benefits resulting from the financing of a particular service or activity? The success of this technique depends on one's ability to identify and quantify as many tangible and intangible costs/benefits as possible. Results are expressed in terms of *benefit*.

cost effectiveness Or cost effectiveness analysis, an analytic approach in which resources/procedures used to support a particular objective actually can or do contribute to that objective's realization; an input-output analysis expressed in terms of *effectiveness*.

cost-of-education index Cost to a school district of preselected goods and services (e.g., teachers, equipment) compared to the average cost of these same goods and services paid by all school districts.

cost-of-living adjustment Adjustment to one's salary that increases or decreases in direct proportion to the cost of living. The measure frequently used for this purpose is the Bureau of Labor Statistics Consumer Price Index. See *COLA*.

cost-quality relationship A premise, introduced by Paul Mort and Francis Cornell, which holds that expenditures for education and quality of education are directly related. Subsequent research has revealed that such a relationship does frequently exist, though not always; further, that improved education does not always follow increases in school expenditures.

cost sharing That portion of the total cost that a grant recipient must pay to fund a project. The recipient's share frequently ranges from 1% to 50%; so-called "in-kind" contributions of materials, facilities, and services may sometimes be made in lieu of actual dollar contributions.

Council of Chief State School Officers (CSSO) Organization made up of state superintendents and commissioners of education in the 50 states and territories. CSSO is an independent council founded in 1928.

Council of Educational Facility Planners (CEFP) An international organization of individuals and groups engaged in the planning, designing, building, maintaining, or equipping of school facilities.

county district A school district whose boundaries are coterminous with those of a county. A city located within a county frequently has its own autonomous school system.

coupon bond A bond to which coupons are attached. These indicate the amount of interest to be paid on the date specified on the coupon.

course Formal instruction covering a specified and organized body of subject matter, presented systematically to students over an extended period of time.

course of study Written guide, prepared by one or more professionals, that serves as an aid to teaching. The guide is normally: (1) limited to a particular academic subject, or part thereof, and (2) designed for use with a particular grade level or type of student.

courseware Instructional materials (i.e., those that teach the learner). Of late, the term appears to be used most frequently in the context of computer-based education.

CPEA See *Cooperative Program in Educational Administration.*

creativity An individual quality with which one is endowed, characterized by behaviors such as inventiveness, a "divergent" mode of thinking, originality, and spontaneous flexibility.

credential Term sometimes used as a synonym for "certificate," "license," or "permit" generally issued by a state agency.

credit (1) Academic credit awarded upon successful completion of a course; may be expressed as a semester hour of credit, a quarter hour of credit, a Carnegie unit, or simply "credit." (2) In bookkeeping, the opposite of debit; an entry reflecting a transaction that decreases assets/expenditure accounts or increases liability, fund balance, or revenue accounts.

criterion A standard. In education, a measure used to evaluate a behavior, test, or program.

criterion-referenced test Or mastery test, an examination consisting of specified minimal performance standards; a test that measures what one should know or be able to do. See *norm-referenced test*.

critic teacher See *cooperating teacher*.

critical incident Personnel technique developed by John Flanagan that elicits descriptions of incidents reflecting competence or incompetence on the part of an individual job-holder. The technique is sometimes used to formulate tests of proficiency or job requirements.

critical path method (CPM) A type of network analysis. Work activities are planned and sequenced for carrying out a project. Various paths are depicted graphically; the one that takes the longest time to complete is the "critical path." Scheduling requirements and cost normally determine which path is ultimately chosen for implementation. See *slack*.

crude birth rate General demographic measure calculated by dividing total births by total population. The resulting quotient is then multiplied by 100 to determine *births per thousand population.*

cultural electives One of two curriculum components included in the Dual Progress Plan, a demonstration program that featured academic departmentalization in the elementary school. The cultural electives block was comprised of mathematics, science, art, and music. See *cultural imperatives* and *Dual Progress Plan*.

cultural imperatives One of two curriculum components included in the Dual Progress Plan, a demonstration program that featured academic departmentalization in the elementary school. This component was considered to be the body of common learnings (academic imperatives) that need to be mastered if one is to function effectively in our culture. The cultural imperatives were English and social studies. See *cultural electives* and *Dual Progress Plan*.

cumulative record A continuous record containing information about a student and his/her progress through the school system. Information retained in the record usually includes: (1) standardized measures (e.g., achievement, I.Q.); (2) personality data; (3) selected health and physical data; (4) family information; (5) attendance data; and (6) grades earned.

current assets Cash, or that which is likely to be turned into cash within a reasonably short period of time (usually within one year).

current dollars Dollar amounts that have not been adjusted to eliminate the effects of inflation.

current expenditures per pupil in ADA Current expenditures in a particular school term divided by the average daily attendance of full-time pupils (or full-time equivalency of pupils) during that term. See *average daily attendance* and *current expenditures*.

current expenditures per pupil in ADM Current expenditures in a particular school term divided by the average daily membership of full-time pupils (or full-time equivalency of pupils) during that term. See *average daily membership* and *current expenditures*.

current expense Any expenditure, whether paid or unpaid, exclusive of capital outlay or debt service.

current funds Funds received during the current year or from reappropriated surpluses. Such funds can be used to pay current obligations.

current liabilities Near-term debts, normally those payable within a year or less.

current ratio Or quick ratio, the relationship between current assets and current liabilities (i.e., the mathematical relationship between that which is owned and that which is owed). See *current assets* and *current liabilities*.

curriculum Varied learning experiences provided under school supervision. Some authorities define it more strictly, applying the term to intended learning outcomes. Others assign a broader connotation to the word and use it to mean the total life experiences of a learner.

curtailed session An abbreviated school session made up of fewer than the minimum number of hours of instruction recommended/required by the state education agency.

cybernetics Science concerned with information control and intercommunication between machines that handle information and man.

D

Dalton Plan A widely adopted and adapted organizational plan for the elementary school, introduced in 1919, that contained these features: (1) individual job sheets (contracts) for each student that were made up of 20 units of work; (2) separate contracts for each subject in the curriculum; (3) three instructional levels (minimum, medium, maximum); and (4) teacher specialists.

damages Monetary awards by the courts for injuries done or suffering sustained. Most common are: (1) "compensatory damages," for lost salary, medical bills, and the like; (2) "punitive damages," awards that exceed the cost of damages actually sustained and are designed to deter similar actions in the future; and (3) "nominal damages," token (symbolic) awards granted when the exact dollar loss is not clearly demonstrated.

dame schools Seventeenth-century New England schools operated on a tuition basis. Young children were taught in private homes by owners or mothers. Instruction consisted principally of reading, ciphering, and religion.

data bank Centralized information depository that contains a comprehensive collection of data, usually in machine-usable form (e.g., tapes, discs); a "superfile." In school systems, these typically contain information relating to budget, personnel, and students.

data base Centralized information depository or master file containing information that is: (1) applicable to a user's needs, and (2) available when needed. Increased use of data processing has expedited the development of data bases.

data processing Any group of people and/or machines that are organized and act together to process information. Such processing includes, but is not limited to specific steps including the recording, sorting, or tabulating of data. Synonymous with information processing.

day care center Professionally managed center that cares for pre-Kindergarten children whose mothers work. Educational experiences are usually included in center programs.

day school A school attended by children during part of the daylight hours; contrasts with a residential school where students study and are boarded on a 24 hours-per-day basis.

de facto segregation Segregation of students by race or ethnic background through forces other than governmental laws or regulations (e.g., neighborhood composition).

de jure segregation Segregation of students by race or ethnic background as the result of intentional governmental action; segregation sanctioned by law or public policy. See *de facto segregation*.

deadwood In organizations, employees who perform at an unsatisfactory level and demonstrate little potential for promotion.

deaf Hearing impairment so severe as to: (1) prevent a student from processing linguistic information through hearing, with or without amplification, and (2) impede educational performance. Also known as nonfunctional hearing.

deaf-blind One with both hearing and visual impairments. Deaf-blind students have communication and educational problems so severe that they can not be accommodated in special classes solely for the deaf or the blind.

debenture bond See *unsecured bond*.

debit In bookkeeping, the column on the left (the credit column is on the right) in which are recorded transactions that indicate the following: (1) asset increase; (2) liability decrease; (3) proprietorship decrease; (4) income decrease; and (5) expense increase. Derived from the Latin word "debeo" (to owe).

debt In school business administration, money owed; a financial obligation resulting from the borrowing of money or from purchases made.

School system debts include bonds, notes, time warrants, and floating debt.

debt limit The maximum amount of gross or net debt permitted by law.

debt service Expenditures for: (1) debt retirement, and (2) interest on debt. Principal and interest of current loans are not included.

debt service fund A special fund created for the purpose of meeting payments on a school system's general obligation debt. Accumulated monies are used to make required principal and interest payments. (Sometimes referred to as a sinking fund.)

debureaucratization Defined by S.N. Eisenstadt to mean the activities by organization members and/or other interested parties that: (1) minimize (sometimes subvert) the goals and rules of a bureaucracy, and (2) serve the interests of those performing such activities. The resultant of this process may be new bureaucratic goals/rules or even a complete takeover of the bureaucracy's activities by other individuals or organizations. See *bureaucratization*.

decentralization Internal administrative reorganization that results in delegation of authority from a higher administrative level to one lower in the hierarchy. In school systems, decentralization is illustrated when authority for functions formerly associated with the central office is assigned to local school principals and their faculties.

decertification (1) A collective bargaining term referring to withdrawal, by an appropriate governmental unit, of an organization's official recognition as sole negotiating representative. (2) Revocation of a teaching or administrative credential by a state following appropriate due process procedures and establishment of just cause for such action. (3) Removal of a student from special education services.

decision-making A problem-solving process in which a problem is analyzed and a solution is chosen after all possible options have been considered. The process is completed once the chosen solution has been implemented.

decision-making, heuristic See *heuristic decision-making*.

decision package See *zero-base budgeting*.

decision unit See *zero-base budgeting*.

decoding The interpretation of a communication.

decremental budgeting A budgeting process in which annual decrements (i.e., decreases) are subtracted from the preceding year's budget; the opposite of incremental budgeting. See *incremental budgeting*.

dedication In the context of school plant planning, a formal ceremony in which a board of education or other agency accepts a new building from a contractor.

defamation Statement(s) to a third party that tend(s) to injure a person's reputation or character. Written/printed defamation is libel; spoken defamation is slander. A tort. See *libel, slander,* and *tort*.

deferred maintenance Property maintenance not performed on schedule (i.e., delayed). As a consequence, the unmaintained property deteriorates and its value decreases.

deinstitutionalization The practice of transferring handicapped individuals from residential institutions to community settings (e.g., halfway houses), one consistent with the mainstreaming and least restrictive environment movements in education. See *least restrictive environment* and *mainstreaming*.

delegation The assignment of duties, and the conferring of authority necessary to carry them out, made by an administrator to a subordinate. The subordinate is thereafter accountable for the satisfactory execution of the duties assigned. See *decentralization*.

deliberate speed Expression used by the United States Supreme Court (*Brown v. Board of Education of Topeka II*, 1955) requiring racial desegregation of schools in the shortest time possible.

delinquent taxes Taxes not paid when due.

Delphi technique A method of collecting independent opinions from a selected number of knowledgeable individuals using successive questionnaires. Instruments are mailed to the selected population. Respondents assign a weighting or priority to their respective responses. These are then collected, clarified, and refined by the data collector and then returned for further responses. Eventually, consensus is reached without the necessity of face-to-face interaction.

demand schedule Schedule based on student needs and interests.

demands Negotiation proposals; items suggested/requested by an employees' organization, or the employer, for inclusion in a new contract (agreement) that is being negotiated.

democratic leadership One of three commonly recognized types of leadership ("democratic" vs. "laissez-faire" vs. "autocratic") identified by Kurt Lewin and his colleagues in 1939. Major characteristics of this type of leadership are shared decision-making, cooperative planning, and open communication. See *autocratic leadership* and *laissez-faire leadership*.

demography Scientific study of human populations; the reporting and analyses of birth, death, and migration rates as well as changes in population sizes, composition, and distribution.

demonstration teaching A form of modeling in which a supervisor, professor, or experienced teacher demonstrates effective teaching methods, proper use of instructional materials, and/or specific instructional strategies for the benefit of one or more teachers or teachers-to-be.

demotion The opposite of promotion. In personnel administration, a form of reassignment that results in a decrease in any or all of the following: income, responsibilities, status, and opportunity. When used in the context of student assignment, demotion means change of a student's placement from a higher to a lower grade level.

density index A student transportation measure computed for comparative purposes; the quotient derived after dividing the total number of students transported by the total number of miles of public roads in a school district.

Department of Superintendence Forerunner organization to the current American Association of School Administrators (AASA). The National Association of School Superintendents became the Department of School Superintendence of the National Education Association in 1870 and, subsequently (1907), the Department of Superintendence of the National Education Association. That name was retained until 1937.

departmentalization The creation of organizational subunits according to purpose/function. In secondary schools and colleges, academic departments are usually organized by subject field with teachers serving as subject specialists and students assigned to more than one teacher (i.e., one instructor for each academic subject).

dependent school district See *fiscally dependent school district*.

deposition A law term; testimony that is taken outside of court but in accordance with court-established procedures. Once recorded by a court stenographer, a deposition is equivalent in value to testimony taken during a formal court proceeding.

depreciation (1) Reduction (decrease) in the value of an asset. Factors contributing to this loss of value include time (obsolescence), usage (wear and tear), and action of the physical elements. (2) When used as an accounting term, depreciation refers to a method for converting fixed assets into expenses over a period of time.

descriptive scale A type of rating scale that makes use of descriptive terms to evaluate one's ability relative to some performance standard (e.g., "well below average," "below average," "average," "above average," "well above average"). See *checklist* and *numerical scale*.

desegregated school A school possessing any or all of the following racial characteristics: (1) enrolls students of two or more races; (2) recently changed from being a single-race to being a biracial institution; and/or (3) has a racially balanced student body. See *racial balance*.

desegregation The bringing together of individuals formerly separated along racial or ethnic lines using some agreed-upon formula. School desegregation is achieved when racially/ethnically different students (and teachers) are assigned to the same schools. See *integration, racial*.

Detroit X-Y-Z Plan An ability grouping plan introduced in 1919. Based on intelligence test scores, students were assigned to one of three ability tracks: X, Y, or Z.

developmental supervision A supervisory approach which recognizes that teachers move from one maturational career level (or stage) to another. Carl D. Glickman has devised a simple teacher development model with stages ranging from "concern with self adequacy" (egocentric) to "concern with students and other teachers" (altruistic). Appropriate models of supervision are recommended for each stage.

deviation I.Q. (D.I.Q.) Standard score on an intelligence test based on the deviation (i.e., difference) between an individual's score and the average score computed for persons of his/her chronological age. Most DIQ's are normally distributed with a mean score of 100 and a standard deviation of 16.

dial access Or random access, a computer-related term that refers to the recording of information in such a way that any piece of data can be retrieved regardless of where it may be stored.

differential See *salary differential*.

differentiated diplomas System of multiple diplomas with type of diploma reflecting the curriculum completed. In larger secondary schools, for example, a variety of diplomas may be conferred: Academic, Vocational, General, Commercial, or Certificate of Attendance.

differentiated staffing The practice of assigning teachers to an instructional team whose members perform different roles and carry different titles (e.g., aide, teacher, master teacher). Status and financial rewards are also differentiated.

diffusion The process by which an innovation is spread and eventually adopted by others.

diploma Document conferred by an educational institution attesting to satisfactory completion of a program of studies. See *differentiated diplomas*.

D.I.Q. See *deviation I.Q.*

direct costs Expenses that can be specifically associated with a particular program, activity, or organizational unit and are distinguishable from indirect costs. See *indirect costs*.

direct services Activities that: (1) are directly related to an organization's function or product, and (2) can be identified with a specific program. Examples: instruction is a direct service related to learning; psychological counseling is a direct service related to mental health. See *supporting services*.

disability Physical or mental condition preventing a student or employee from carrying out part or all of his/her assigned duties. Such incapacity is of several types: (1) temporary partial; (2) permanent partial; (3) temporary total; and (4) permanent total.

disbursement Broadly speaking, a form of payment; money paid out or spent. Synonymous with "expenditure" when used in the context of school budgeting.

discrepancy evaluation A type of program evaluation in which actual performance is compared against a predetermined standard (i.e., expectation). Differences noted, or "discrepancies," are used to change either the program or the standard.

discretionary duty A duty that permits the administrator to exercise discretion when executing his official responsibilities; the opposite of ministerial duty. See *ministerial duty*.

discretionary funds Generally small funds available to individual administrators for incidental expenditures. At the school building level, discretionary funds may have their origins in sources such as parent groups, fund-raising activities, and gifts.

discrimination The intended or unintended denial of equal opportunity to an individual because of his/her race, religion, age, sex, national origin, or color.

disengagement One of four *teacher behavior* dimensions (subtests) included in the OCDQ. Disengagement describes the faculty member who, while "going through the motions" as a teacher, tends to function in a detached fashion (i.e., tends not to be an active, integrated member of the total school operation). See *Organizational Climate Description Questionnaire*.

disfunctional behavior In organizations, the intended or unintended behavior of individuals that disrupts normal routines and/or thwarts realization of the organization's goals.

dismissal In school personnel administration, the termination of a tenured teacher's employment. Such termination may take place at any point during the year but is subject to due process procedures prescribed by law. Not a synonym for "nonrenewal." See *nonrenewal*.

dissatisfiers One of two motivation classifications, identified by Frederick Herzberg, that relate to job performance. According to Herzberg's research, the factors making up the "dissatisfier" category are organizational policy and administration, supervision, salary, interpersonal relations, job security, and working conditions. See *satisfiers*.

distributive bargaining Negotiations carried out for the purpose of determining how relatively scarce items are to be allocated within an organization.

district power equalizing (DPE) An approach to school financing that equalizes educational opportunity for all public school students. The key feature of DPE is that the state guarantees a certain expenditure level per student; in the case of "poor" school districts, the state makes up the difference between moneys raised locally and the guarantee level established.

division of labor Organizational practice of assigning specialized tasks to different organizational members. Task assignments are made on the basis of individual factors such as ability, skill, experience, and training.

double entry A system of bookkeeping that involves at least two accounts. For every entry made in the debit side of an account, a like amount is entered as a credit in another account. This shows the effect of each transaction on assets, liabilities, and proprietorship.

double sessions The assigning of two different groups of children to the same classroom but at different times of the day (e.g., AM and PM), an arrangement that normally results in shortened school days for both groups. This approach to pupil assignment is necessitated when the number of students to be accommodated exceeds the number of teaching stations available.

dress code Written regulations prescribing the appropriate dress and personal appearance of students and/or teachers.

dropout A previously enrolled student who: (1) leaves school voluntarily before completing a program of studies, or qualifying for graduation, and (2) does not register in any other school. Such departure may take place while school is in session or between terms.

dual enrollment See *shared time*.

dual executive control Term used to describe organizations headed by two chief executive officers who are coordinate in rank. Illustrating such organizations is the school system employing a separate school superintendent and a separate school business administrator, each reporting independently and directly to the board of education. See *unit executive control.*

dual marking plan A student grading system that provides two marks: one for the student's achievement relative to other students (i.e., some form of norms), the other relative to the individual student's ability.

Dual Progress Plan Demonstration program, conceived by George D. Stoddard and funded by the Ford Foundation; featured academic departmentalization in the elementary school, specialist teaching, and nongraded advancement in mathematics, science, music, and art. Curriculum was divided into two blocks: cultural imperatives and cultural electives. The demonstration was conducted in two New York school systems: Ossining and Long Beach. See *cultural electives* and *cultural imperatives.*

dual school system School system with predominantly white and predominantly black student bodies, each physically separated from the other.

dual supervision Situation that prevails when a member of an organization is responsible to two superiors (e.g., the classroom teacher who reports concurrently to a building principal and a subject supervisor); a condition violative of the unity of command principle. See *unity of command.*

due process Procedural safeguard, established to protect individuals from actions of an arbitrary, capricious, or unreasonable nature—this in keeping with the Fourteenth and other Amendments of the Constitution. Due process guarantees the individual the right to a fair hearing (trial). See *due process clause, procedural due process,* and *substantive due process.*

due process clause That part of the 14th Amendment to the U.S. Constitution reading: "...nor shall any state deprive any person of life, liberty, or property without due process of law."

duties Tasks/functions that a member of an organization is required to perform in order to continue his/her place in the organizational structure. See *discretionary duty* and *ministerial duty.*

duty, discretionary See *discretionary duty.*

duty, ministerial See *ministerial duty.*

dynamic equilibrium Systems theory term used to describe a shifting of organizational goals, or even a rearrangement of the organization per se, for the purpose of accommodating change(s) in the organization's environment. Balance between the organization and its environment is thus achieved. See *static equilibrium.*

E

early childhood education (1) Education for young children offered at the primary and preprimary levels. (2) Professional programs that prepare primary and preprimary level teachers.

early departure Leaving school prior to the official close of the school day.

education code See *school code*.

Education for All Handicapped Act. See *Public Law 94-142*.

Education for All Handicapped Children Act See *Public Law 94-142*.

Educational Administration Abstracts Abstracts of articles dealing with educational administration that have appeared in educational and behavioral science journals; a quarterly publication of the University Council for Educational Administration.

Educational Administration Quarterly Publication of the University Council for Educational Administration; contains original articles dealing with matters such as research relevant to educational leadership, policy matters, and theoretical papers.

educational equity Principle that all students, regardless of race, sex, age, national origin, social class, or handicap, are entitled to equal educational opportunities; nondiscriminatory educational treatment.

Educational Facilities Laboratory (EFL) A division of the Academy for Educational Development, and formerly an independent foundation, that: (1) encourages school plant planning research; (2) assists educational institutions with physical problems; and (3) disseminates information relating to school facilities.

educational overburden School finance term referring to the extra funds required by some school districts enrolling a disproportionately large number of handicapped or disadvantaged students, or those for whom English is not a native language.

educational parks Single campuses (usually urban) on which are situated schools of all levels—elementary, middle, and senior high school. Major purpose of this arrangement is to foster better integration of students by bringing all students, representing all races and social classes, to the common site.

educational record Or student record, a file, maintained by a school or an agent of the school, that contains information about one or more students.

Educational Research Service (ERS) Nonprofit agency, sponsored by seven school management and policy organizations, that provides school leaders with timely research and information. Publishes special study reports and also maintains an "on-call service" for member administrators/school board members seeking specific information.

Educational Resources Information Center (ERIC) A national information system, operated by the National Institute of Education, that provides ready access to research and development efforts, descriptions of examplary programs, and other useful educational information.

educational specifications Written descriptions of learning activities to be carried out in a school. These are prepared to help the school architect to design a building whose facilities will meet program needs.

Educational Testing Service (ETS) Nonprofit organization, headquartered in Princeton, NJ, dedicated to measurement and research. ETS' standardized examinations, such as the Scholastic Aptitude Test, the Graduate Record Examination, and the National Teachers Examination, are used widely in the United States.

educationally deprived child Child who requires special (i.e., compensatory) instruction/assistance for the purpose of raising a relatively low level of educational achievement. Deprived children include those who are handicapped or whose educational deficiency results from poverty, neglect, delinquency, or cultural/linguistic separation. See *compensatory education*.

effective synergy See *synergy*.

effectiveness A systems management concern with goal realization. Effectiveness is a measure of the disparity between expectations and performance, or the extent to which an output accords with a stated goal. See *efficiency*.

efficiency The realization of goals with the optimal investment of time, energy, and cost. Efficiency is realized when a particular method, compared with other possible methods, results in the realization of quality goals and, in doing so, requires fewer of these investments. See *effectiveness*.

Eight Year Study National experiment, involving graduates of 30 experimental high schools, sponsored by the Progressive Education Association (1933-1941). Investigators concluded that students from high schools with innovative programs fared as well, or better, in college as did their matched counterparts from high schools with traditional programs.

elementary school A school classified as an elementary school by the state; one including any span of grades up through grade 8. Common grade spans are K–5 or K–6.

elementary school district School system that operates elementary schools only.

eleven-month plan Proposal that would create an eleven-month school year in contrast to the standard nine-month year. This arrangement, if implemented, would permit students to complete their regular twelve years of study in ten years.

elites A term sometimes used when referring to formal or informal leaders in an organization who have power. Individuals in a society considered to be the most influential, powerful, prestigious, and/or the most superior.

Elizabeth Plan Plan for organizing elementary school pupils, introduced into the Elizabeth, New Jersey schools (1895) by William J. Shearer. Three or four achievement sections were created within each grade level. Students advanced within their respective sections, or from grade to grade, whenever ready for advanced work (regardless of time of year).

emancipated minor A minor who, legally, is self-sufficient, free from parental or guardian control, and has no intention of returning to his/her parents' residence. Emancipated minors: (1) are free to choose their own residence or domicile, and (2) may, where legal residence has been established, attend school within a school district on a tuition-free (resident) basis.

emergent leadership Leadership exercised by someone in a group other than a status (officially designated) leader. Such leadership tends to "emerge" as the group faces some new problem or social situation.

emeritus Title of distinction conferred on a male professional (frequently an academician) at the time of retirement (e.g., professor emeritus). Female variation: emerita.

eminent domain The right of a governmental unit (e.g., school district) to take private property for public use. The governmental unit is obligated: (1) to demonstrate that the property is needed, and (2) to pay a fair price to the owner. The price paid may be negotiated or fixed by a court of law.

employee evaluation system See *evaluation system*.

encounter group Group therapy experience that attempts to help group members to: (1) become more aware of themselves; (2) attempt new behaviors; and (3) develop new and more relaxed interpersonal skills. Participants are encouraged to experiment with new behaviors; each receives feedback on his/her behavior.

encumbrances Financial obligations chargeable to an appropriation; commitments to purchase something. Examples are purchase orders, salary commitments, or other contracts. These obligations cease to be encumbrances when paid or when the actual liability has been satisfied.

endowment fund A permanent fund whose principal must remain intact. Proceeds from the fund (e.g., interest, dividends) are used for special purposes such as student scholarships or, in higher education, to support a distinguished professorship.

endowment insurance Insurance that pays the policyholder a lump sum upon reaching a certain age. Should the policyholder die before then, a death benefit is payable to the designated beneficiary.

enrollment The total number of students registered in a school or school system.

entrance rate The hourly rate paid to newly-hired employees. In education, such rates almost always apply to certain noncertificated personnel.

entropy Concept, derived from communication theory, that describes a tendency toward disorder, disorganization, inactivity, or even chaos in an established system. Such condition can frequently be attributed to the system's failure to adapt to new stimuli, especially when the magnitude and nature of the stimuli may be unknown.

entrusted authority Authority that is extended to a leader by his/her subordinates (e.g., election of a department chairperson). See *vested authority*.

entry In business administration, the record of a financial transaction entered in the designated book of account. Not to be confused with organizational entry. See *organizational entry*.

enumeration See *school census*.

enumeration date The date on which the census (school or general) is taken.

environmental theories Theories suggesting that the emergence of a leader is related to the condition (situation) prevailing in an organization. Environmental theorists hold that situations produce leaders; further, that leaders do not produce situations.

equal employment opportunity An employment safeguard, enforced by federal legislation, which assures all persons, regardless of race, color, creed, sex, or national origin, of equal treatment in areas such as hiring, discharge, tenure, and promotion.

equal protection clause That part of the U.S. Constitution's 14th Amendment, adopted in 1868, which provides that "no State shall . . . deny to any person within its jurisdiction, the equal protection of the laws."

equalization aid Or financial equalization, financial assistance furnished to a school district or other lower-level government by a state or other high-level government for the purpose of reducing significant wealth disparities. Equalization aid to school districts assures that each child will receive a minimum dollar-per-pupil education, an important assurance to students residing in "poor" districts.

equifinality Social systems concept suggesting that, in organizations, final results may be achieved using different approaches and different initial conditions.

equilibrium See *dynamic equilibrium*.

equipment Items which (1) are nonexpendable; (2) generally last for a long period of time; (3) retain their original shape and appearance with use; and (4) are more likely to be repaired than replaced if damaged. Examples of equipment are desks, typewriters, and musical instruments.

equity In business administration, the dollar excess of assets over liabilities; also known as fund balance.

equivalency diploma See *Certificate of High School Equivalency*.

ergonomy An industrial concept: the matching of machines to persons, not vice-versa. In education, the procedure that permits professionals (e.g., teachers) to select their own methods/materials, in effect matching these to their own skills/abilities.

ERIC See *Educational Resources Information Center*.

escalator clause Provision in a collective bargaining agreement or pension plan stipulating: (1) that salaries/benefits are to be increased or decreased in accordance with cost-of-living changes, and (2) the index to be used for determining such changes.

esprit (1) Spirit; spriteliness. (2) In the Organizational Climate Description Questionnaire, one of four *teacher behavior* dimensions (subtests) that measures teacher morale. See *Organizational Climate Description Questionnaire*.

estimated life Anticipated number of years that an equipment item or other property will function satisfactorily.

ETS See *Educational Testing Service.*

evaluation The appraisal of results, events, or behaviors in terms of predetermined goals or objectives. The act of comparing desired outcomes with actual outcomes; a measure of effectiveness or efficiency.

Evaluative Criteria Printed guide for faculty members engaged in a self-study of their school. Published by the National Study of School Evaluation, this booklet is used extensively by schools preparing for regional accreditation.

ex officio membership Membership eligibility on a board, committee, or other body that accrues from an office or official position held.

exception principle An organizational principle, enunciated by Frederick W. Taylor, which holds that policies should be developed so that responsibility for resolution of recurring problems can be delegated; further, that the superior should deal only with the exceptional problem.

exceptional child A child who requires special educational planning and services by virtue of marked mental, emotional, physical, social, or sensory deviation(s) from group norms. Talented and gifted children are usually included in this definition.

exceptionality A significant deviation from group norms. In special education, the term refers to physical, health, psychological, sensory, mental, or proficiency characteristics markedly different from those of others in the same age group.

excess cost Cost difference between average annual expenditures per student and the larger per-pupil expenditures required to educate an exceptional child. See *exceptional child.*

exchange theories Theories based on the idea that members of an organization make contributions to it at some cost to themselves in exchange for which they receive rewards of some type (e.g., monetary, satisfaction). The exchange process remains ongoing so long as group members find it to be a satisfying one.

excise tax A tax levied on certain commodities. Among the best-known excise taxes are those levied against tobacco, gasoline, and liquor.

exclusive representative The one employee organization designated to represent employees for negotiations with the employer.

Executive Professional Leadership (EPL) A term coined by researchers Neal Gross and Robert Herriott as part of their study of the elementary principalship. They used it to mean "the effort of an executive of a professionally staffed organization to conform to a definition of his role that stresses his obligation to improve the quality of staff performance" (*Executive Professional Leadership*, p. 22).

executive session Meeting of a school board or other legislative body from which the public is excluded. Only those persons specifically invited by the board are permitted to be present. State laws frequently limit executive sessions to certain topics (e.g., personnel matters). See *sunshine laws*.

exempt positions Positions whose incumbents (usually professional and managerial employees) are exempt from legislation requiring payment of overtime.

exempted child A child who, although of compulsory school age, is not required to attend school because no program exists that meets his/her unique educational need(s).

exit interview Interview conducted with an employee at the time he/she is being separated from the organization (e.g, retirement, resignation). This interview serves several purposes: (1) matters requiring attention are identified; (2) ideas and impressions are exchanged; and (3) role evaluation takes place.

expectancy theories of motivation Theories which focus upon rational behavior and anticipated outcomes. The best known of these, proffered by Victor Vroom, suggests that an individual employee's motivation results from his/her belief that increased job performance will result in certain rewards (e.g., promotion, salary increase).

expenditures Charges incurred in a particular fiscal year, whether or not paid; decreases in net financial resources.

expert power The power which an individual enjoys because of his/her perceived high level of expertise; one of five classifications of power developed by John R.P. French, Jr. and Bertram Raven. See *coercive power, legitimate power, referent power,* and *reward power*.

express contract A type of contract, frequently contrasted with "implied contract," in which the rights and duties of the parties to the contract are stated expressly, either in written form or orally. See *implied contract*.

expulsion Action, taken by a school board in accordance with prescribed due process procedures, compelling a student to withdraw from school, permanently or substantially so, for violating a valid school rule. Due process procedures normally require that a formal hearing be held. Valid rules are those that protect the health, safety, and welfare of students or preclude serious disruption of a school's operation.

extended family A family that includes three or more generations; a composite family made up of two or more nuclear families. See *nuclear family*.

extended school day That part of the calendar day, following the regular session, when school-sponsored activities (e.g., club meetings, recreational events, rehearsals) take place.

extended school year See *year-round school*.

external evaluation Appraisal conducted by individuals who are not involved in the program or procedure under review. External evaluators usually come from outside the organization and are engaged on an ad hoc basis.

extra-curricular activities See *cocurricular activities*.

extrinsic motivation See *motivation*.

F

facility Land, a building, or a part of a building; something designed, constructed, or installed to perform a specific function.

factfinding Investigation of an employer-employee dispute by an officially designated individual or panel. Factfinders submit reports of the facts and issues involved once all evidence has been collected and studied. They frequently make public recommendations intended to resolve the dispute.

factor analysis Any of several statistical methods employed to explain or account for the intercorrelations among several variables (including tests). Ideally, the number of hypothetical (explaining) "factors" is smaller than the number of variables.

faculty In schools, a distinction is frequently made between "faculty" and "staff." Faculty consists of all teachers, librarians, assistant principals, guidance workers, etc.; staff, on the other hand, refers to all other school personnel such as secretaries, bus drivers, custodians, and cafeteria workers.

fair share See *agency fee*.

familiar climate One of six *organizational climates* identified through use of the OCDQ. Familiar climate schools scored as follows on OCDQ subtests: (1) high "disengagement"; (2) low "hindrance"; (3) average "esprit"; (4) high "intimacy"; (5) high "consideration"; (6) low "aloofness"; (7) low "production emphasis"; and (8) average "thrust." See *Organizational Climate Description Questionnaire*.

family Group of people with common ancestors; a basic kinship unit. More specifically, a unit made up of a household head and one or more others in the same household who are related to the head. See *extended family* and *nuclear family*.

feasibility study Analysis undertaken to determine: (1) the suitability and practicality of a new system or program, or alternatives thereto and (2) its likelihood of success.

Federal Register A publication issued every weekday by the U.S. General Services Administration. It lists federal agency regulations and legal notices, including information about federal grants competitions.

fee In education, a charge or compensation for services, privileges, or the use of specialized equipment or facilities; excludes cost of instruction.

feedback Procedures built into a system that compare actual performance with planned performance. Such information is used to determine what corrective steps, if any, need to be taken to achieve goals. Data processors define feedback as that part of a closed loop system which automatically reports back about the condition under control.

fenestration An architectural term referring to the positioning of windows such that natural light is provided to the interior of a building.

fertility rate Or general fertility rate, demographic measure computed by multiplying 1,000 times the number of births in a year, divided by the number of females (ages 15–44).

fidelity bond A bond that guarantees a school system or other employers against losses that result from the actions of selected employees or other individuals (e.g., treasurer) associated with the system.

financial equalization See *equalization aid*.

FIRO See *Fundamental Interpersonal Relations Orientation*.

fiscal year That twelve-month period, usually July 1 through June 30, for which a school district's budget is prepared. At the close of the fiscal year, the district's books are closed and its financial condition is ascertained.

fiscally dependent school district A district whose board of education is legally required to have its school budget or tax levy approved by some other governmental authority (e.g., a city council). See *fiscally independent school district*.

fiscally independent school district A district whose board of education is legally authorized to: (1) prepare its own school budget, and (2) levy the taxes necessary to support that budget. See *fiscally dependent school district*.

fixed asset Capital asset, tangible or intangible, that is durable and long-lasting. Tangible assets include items such as buildings, machinery, and furniture. Intangible assets consist primarily of patents, copyrights, and goodwill.

fixed charges Classification used in financial accounting for expenditures that recur fairly regularly. Included are items such as rents, insurance, interest on current loans, and contributions to retirement programs.

fixed cost A cost that remains relatively constant (e.g., rent, an insurance premium) over a period of time. Such costs normally remain constant even as program or activity changes may be made.

fixed limits marking plan Grading system sometimes used in schools whose students are grouped by ability. The plan restricts academic grade ranges for each group. Students in a high ability group, for example, may earn grades of A, B, or C; those in the middle group, grades ranging from B–F; and those in the low group, grades ranging from C to F.

Flanders interaction analysis See *interaction analysis*.

flat grant A form of state assistance in which the state pays a fixed amount to a school district using some uniform unit of measure such as "x" dollars for each full-time teacher or "y" dollars for each student in average daily attendance. Because the state's per-unit allocation is the same for each school district, variations in district wealth notwithstanding, a flat grant can not be considered to be equalization aid.

flat organization A formal organization with relatively few authority levels separating the lowest and highest level employees. Organizational distance between these two levels, measured hierarchically, is short, thus creating a "flat" table of organization. See *tall organization*.

flexible schedule An instructional schedule that differs from a traditional schedule in three respects: (1) class sizes may vary from course to course; (2) lengths of class periods are not uniform; and (3) the number of class meetings per week vary from one course to another.

floating holiday A holiday observable at a time chosen by the individual employee rather than on officially designated holidays.

floating schedule A nonconventional student schedule that includes one class period that "floats" (i.e., meets at different times each day, or may not convene daily).

flow chart Graphic (diagram) that indicates the steps required to complete a specific task or to solve a problem. Symbols are used to indicate information such as: (1) data to be used; (2) action steps to be taken; and (3) work flow.

flow-through monies Funds (e.g., federal funds) which a state agency, serving as an intermediary, distributes. These funds are neither a receipt or an expenditure insofar as the distributing agency is concerned.

Follow Through Federally supported program, introduced in 1967, to reinforce early intervention programs, notably Head Start, through various educational and health projects designed and carried out at the local level.

followership Cooperativeness with the leader exhibited by his/her subordinates.

food services Service activities, carried out by a school or school system, associated with the preparation and distribution of lunches, snacks, or special meals that are school related.

force field analysis A model, originated by Kurt Lewin, for analyzing organizational change. Lewin held that two sets of environmental forces operate to keep an organization in a state of equilibrium. They are: (1) *driving forces,* those that promote change, and (2) *restraining forces,* those that resist it. Lewin's three-step proposal for producing change consists of: (1) unfreezing (i.e., disrupting the equilibrium); (2) changing; and (3) refreezing.

foreseeability In law, the ability or obligation to anticipate (foresee) harm. For example, a student injury attributable to a teacher's failure to foresee danger to the student may result in the teacher being charged with negligence.

formal authority See *legitimate power.*

formal communication In organizations, the process through which official information is transmitted, office-to-office or position-to-position, via explicit communication channels. Example: a written memorandum that a building principal addresses to his/her school's faculty. See *communication* and *informal communication.*

formal organization A structured, hierarchically arranged, social system made up of individuals who perform separate yet interrelated and consciously coordinated functions, with rules, goals, and leaders of its own. Examples of a formal organization are: a school system, a bank, and the army. The official blueprint of an organization, describing the organization as it should be.

formative evaluation An assessment carried out during the course of a program or project. Contrasts with "summative evaluations" which are assessments carried out after a program or project has been completed. See *summative evaluation.*

formula funding Allocation of funds in accordance with predetermined criteria such as number of students, number of classrooms, or type of curriculum.

FORTRAN Programming language used mainly for scientific, engineering, and mathematical data processing; acronym for *For*mula *Tran*slator.

45-15 plan One of several academic calendar arrangements developed in connection with year-round schooling. Basically a four-quarter system; students attend school for 45 days and then vacation for 15. All students are enrolled during each quarter.

foster home Household in which a child is reared, without adoption, by someone other than its biological parents.

foundation program A financial (equalization) program that guarantees a minimum (foundation) level of revenue support for each student in a state. The procedure for implementing a foundation program involves: (1) establishing a minimum level of support for the state, expressed as revenues-per-child; (2) local taxation at a specified level;

and (3) use of state aid, as necessary, that is the difference between revenues raised locally and the established foundation level.

four-quarter plan One plan for carrying out the concept of year-round education. The plan involves: (1) dividing the calendar year into quarters, and (2) dividing a school's student body into four sections. Each section attends three (rotated) quarters with the result that only 75% of the school's enrollment is in attendance during any quarter.

free, appropriate education Cost-free special education and related services that: (1) are carried out in appropriate, usually public schools, and (2) conform with state standards and Public Law 94-142.

frequency distribution Or distribution of scores, a tabulation of scores (or cases) arranged into "intervals," or orderly groupings that range from *highest* to *lowest*. The number of scores falling within each interval is recorded beside each. Example:

Interval	*N (frequency)*
95–99	3
90–94	5
85–89	8
80–84	7

fringe benefits A general term used in personnel administration to describe benefits received by employees in addition to regular salaries. Benefits commonly made available by school districts include sick leave, life insurance, hospitalization insurance, and a retirement plan. See *perquisites*.

FTE See *full-time equivalency*.

full state funding Or full state assumption (FSA), a school finance plan for funding public elementary and secondary education. The plan proposes that: (1) the state government shall assume full responsibility for funding education, and (2) equal per-pupil expenditures are to be distributed to each of the state's school districts.

full-time equivalency Or FTE, a mathematical measure used to report less than full-time activity. To compute the ratio: divide actual time devoted to an activity by time required in a corresponding full-time activity; express as a decimal, usually to the nearest tenth. FTE is used to measure part-time teaching and administrative activities as well as part-time student enrollments.

functional illiterate An adult who cannot read, write, or compute sufficiently to be able to function effectively in society. One operational definition includes all adults who did not attend school beyond the eighth grade or are unable to read, write, or compute at eighth grade level.

functions (1) Activities/procedures devised to fulfill one or more basic purposes. (2) In personnel administration, the operation(s) that a jobholder is expected to perform. See *latent functions* and *manifest functions*.

fund An independent accounting entity (much like a separate business). Each fund contains a complete and self-balancing record of assets, liabilities, and fund balances. Most school districts operate a "general fund" plus numbers of "special funds," the latter usually established to account for the financing of some specific activity. Examples of "special funds" include debt service, special revenue, and proprietary funds.

fund balance See *equity*.

Fundamental Interpersonal Relations Orientation (FIRO) A trilogy of ways to describe interpersonal relations, formulated by William Schutz. FIRO's three elements are: (1) "power orientation," the tendency to go by the rules; (2) "personalness-counterpersonalness orientation," being attracted to people on the basis of personal liking; and (3) "assertiveness orientation," the inclination to express one's opinion openly.

funded debt See *bonded debt*.

G

game theory A mathematical technique for finding solutions to problems. Conflict situations are presented to two or more players who are then required to identify, select, and test possible strategies. The object is to devise strategies that are superior to those proposed by other players.

Gantt Chart A method, developed by Henry Gantt, for depicting graphically and over a period of time the relationship between planned (scheduled) and actual performance. The graphic is usually presented in horizontal bar form.

garnishment Court order, secured by a creditor, that requires an employer to put aside a specified sum from an employee's wages for the purpose of reducing (repaying) an existing debt.

Gary Plan Organizational plan for the upper elementary grades, introduced in Gary, Indiana in 1919. It featured platooning. Students, as a group, received instruction in one block of subjects (e.g., language and social studies) while a second platoon pursued other special activities. The two platoons reversed positions at some pre-arranged time.

GED See *Certificate of High School Equivalency*.

general administration In education, the overall administrative responsibilities for an entire school system; central administration.

general aid Funds provided by one government to a lower-level government (e.g., aid from the state to a school district). No earmarking of funds is involved; instead, the receiving governing authority may use funds received as it sees fit.

general educational development (GED) program Program of instruction designed to prepare students who plan to take the high school equivalency examination. See *Certificate of High School Equivalency*.

general fertility rate See *fertility rate*.

general fund A fund used by a school district to account for all ordinary transactions not accounted for in another fund. Included are items such as taxes collected, utility costs, salaries paid, state and federal aid received, and tuition.

general ledger At the school district level, a general file or book of records that summarizes, in detail, the district's financial transactions and its financial position.

general obligation bonds Instruments of indebtedness (i.e., bonds) whose payment is pledged by the credit and good faith of the issuing agency. In school districts, payment is usually made from taxes and other general revenues.

general systems theory See *systems theory*.

generalist teacher Instructor who teaches all or most subjects in the curriculum to one group of students, as in a self-contained classroom. See *specialist teacher*.

generic decisions Decisions involving routine and recurring problems for which rules, policies, and regulations have been established. These written guidelines aid the decision-maker responsible for resolving such problems. The "generic decision" vs. "unique decision" typology was formulated by Peter F. Drucker. See *unique decisions*.

gerontology The scientific study of the aged and their problems.

gifted and talented Students whose outstanding ability makes them capable of high performance; includes those with demonstrated achievement or potential ability in any (or combinations) of the following: (1) intellectual ability; (2) a particular academic aptitude; (3) creative thinking; (4) leadership ability; (5) visual or performing arts; and/or (6) psychomotor ability.

goal Statement of broad purpose or aim. Unlike objectives, which are explicitly stated and measurable aims, goals are general statements of intent that can not be measured as stated. Example: "to help students become better citizens." See *objective*.

goal displacement The situation that prevails when the means used by an organization to realize goals become ends in themselves; means and ends become inverted. Characteristic of bureaucracies that: (1) cling to rigid rules and regulations; and (2) are generally unwilling to establish and work toward new goals.

goal identification The process of identifying desired organizational outcomes. Goals are stated in relatively broad terms (e.g., "to improve the quality of instruction") and followed by specific objectives. See *goal*.

good faith Or good-faith negotiation, term used to describe certain positive attitudes which negotiating parties bring with them when meeting to reach a mutually satisfactory agreement. Characteristics of good-faith negotiation are open and free discussions, fairness, and an earnest desire to overcome obstacles to agreement.

governance Control and authority over the decision-making process(es).

gpa See *grade point average*.

grade equivalent The grade level for which a score is the average, expressed in terms of grade level and academic months. For example, a pupil's score on a standardized achievement test may be equivalent to the average score earned by students in the fourth month of the fifth grade. In this case, the grade equivalent is expressed as 5.4.

grade point average Or g.p.a., statistic used to report a student's average academic performance for some specified period of time (e.g., semester, year). When a four-point "quality" system is used ($A=4$, $B=3$, $C=2$, $D=1$), the total number of quality points earned is divided by the total number of credit hours of instruction attempted during the period specified.

graded school A school in which fundamental skills and knowledges to be taught are packaged and arranged, sequentially, into standard instructional levels that normally require one year of instruction. Students are then assigned to an appropriate level, usually on the basis of chronological age.

grant Financial or material award made to an individual, group, or agency whose application/proposal best meets established criteria.

grant administrator The designated individual in an organization who assists local project directors with the development of their respective grant proposals (including budgets) and who may subsequently be required to monitor each funded project to insure that it is being implemented in accordance with grant regulations.

grant-in-aid Financial support from a central government (e.g., federal, state) to a smaller governmental unit such as a school district or local municipality. Funds are normally earmarked for some particular program/activity.

grapevine Informal communication network that is not an official part of the organizational structure; the person-to-person method used by organization members to communicate privileged information and rumors.

great man theory Leadership theory which holds that leadership skill is hereditary (i.e., that leaders are effective because they possess certain biologically superior qualities).

grievance A complaint about working conditions, expressed by an employee, that describes real or perceived injustices, mistreatment, or other forms of personal injury. Such complaints are customarily brought to the attention of management.

grievance procedure A method (plan) for routing/processing of employee grievances. Such procedures are normally described in writing and included as part of collective bargaining agreements.

gross income Revenues before any expenses are deducted. An accounting term; may be applied to individuals as well as institutions.

gross national product (GNP) A method of expressing national income. Expressed in dollar terms, it represents the total value of all goods and services produced by a nation in a given time period (usually one year).

group A small plurality of individuals who have several characteristics in common, including: (1) interdependence; (2) intercommunication; (3) goals; and (4) personal satisfaction derived from group membership. See *primary group* and *secondary group*.

group cohesiveness See *cohesiveness*.

group conflict See *conflict*.

group dynamics A component of social science concerned with factors such as: (1) the nature of groups; (2) group behavior; (3) the interrelationships among group members; and (4) the operational effectiveness of a group.

group insurance Type of insurance that covers homogeneous groups of people, usually employees (and, frequently, their dependents), under a master contract. Coverage is variable, depending on the contract (e.g., life, accidental death and dismemberment, hospital and surgical, dental). Premium rates are usually lower and may be paid by the employer or shared by employer and employee.

group norms See *norms*.

H

half-day session An abbreviated school day, usually comprising half the number of hours prescribed for a full school day and most frequently used at the Kindergarten and pre-Kindergarten levels.

halo effect The tendency of an evaluator to be influenced by one favorable characteristic, trait, or response of a person to such an extent that all other characteristics, traits, or responses are rated similarly.

handicap As defined by many special educators, the problems, disadvantages, and social nonacceptance that result from mental or physical disabilities/deviations. In common usage, a synonym for "disability." See *disability*.

handicapped children As defined in Public Law 94-142, children determined to be mentally retarded, hard of hearing, deaf, speech impaired, visually handicapped, seriously emotionally disturbed, orthopedically impaired, other health impaired, deaf-blind, multi-handicapped, or children with specific learning disabilities, whose impairments require special education and related services.

hard of hearing Individuals with reduced auditory acuity. The sense of hearing is defective, but functional; the condition may be permanent or fluctuating. Not a synonym for "deaf." See *deaf*.

hardware The physical (mechanical) equipment that makes up a computer system, as contrasted with "software." See *software*.

Hawthorne studies Series of industrial psychology experiments carried out by Elton Mayo at a Western Electric Company plant. They were carried out to determine the effect of physical stimuli on employee productivity. Findings showed that: (1) salaries and physical working conditions alone do not influence employee motivation; (2) psychological and social atmosphere (i.e., interpersonal relationships of the workers) have a profound influence on productivity; (3) employee performance improves when they receive the attention and interest of management; and, (4) employees tend to resist change that affects working conditions, especially if imposed from above with minimum information and involvement.

hazing Brutality frequently associated with initiation into a fraternity/sorority or other membership organization. Examples include whipping; forced calisthenics; forced consumption of food, drink, or drugs; physical isolation; forced conduct producing extreme embarrassment; and, sleep deprivation.

Head Start Or Operation Head Start, federally supported program that makes educational enrichment activities as well as health screening and treatment available to economically disadvantaged preschool children.

head teacher In small, usually rural schools, a full-time teacher who, during non-school hours, carries out selected administrative duties. Positions of this type were commonplace prior to the school consolidation movement; few remain today.

headmaster In Britain, the title held by the principal of an elementary or secondary school. In the U.S., the title accorded principals of some private schools. Female variation: headmistress.

health services Noninstructional medical, dental, nursing, and mental health services provided to students.

hearing Legal or quasi-legal oral proceeding in which a court or tribunal hears arguments, witnesses, ideas, or evidence. Hearings conducted for the purpose of collecting evidence are known as trials or trial-like hearings; those that serve to hear ideas are referred to as arguments.

hearing officer Individual officially designated to preside over hearings and to issue reports.

helping teacher A successful teacher who, by virtue of his/her demonstrated instructional ability, is chosen by a school or school system and charged with the task of helping classroom teachers to improve their teaching techniques. Helping teachers (sometimes called consultants) normally do not participate in the evaluation of those whom they are assisting. Helping teachers should not be confused with teacher aides.

Herzberg's theory of motivation See *motivation-hygiene theory*.

heterogeneous grouping Or mixed grouping, the practice of assigning students, dissimilar with respect to ability and/or achievement, to the same group or class; opposite of homogeneous grouping. See *homogeneous grouping*.

heuristic decision-making Stimulating and creative decision-making activity that does not follow the formal table of organization. Instead, the leader encourages open discussion, the generation of fresh ideas/possible solutions, and eventual consensus on the part of individuals who work at different organizational levels.

hidden agenda An agenda or motives with hidden (i.e., nonexplicit) purposes.

hierarchy The administrative subsystem of a school, school system, or other formal organization; individuals who hold high rank and, as a result, have the capacity to exert power and/or enjoy certain privileges.

hierarchy-of-needs theory Motivational theory formulated by Abraham Maslow (1943). Man is described as a wanting animal; as one of his needs is satisfied, another (of a higher level, or hierarchy) takes its place. The hierarchy, low to high, consists of five need levels: (1) physiological; (2) safety; (3) social; (4) ego; and (5) self-fulfillment.

high school district School system that operates secondary schools only.

higher education Post-secondary programs sponsored by public or private institutions of higher education: junior/community colleges, two-year technical institutes, colleges, and universities.

hindrance One of four *teacher behavior* dimensions (subtests) included in the OCDQ. Refers to teachers who perceive the principal as hindering rather than facilitating the work of the teacher by adding undue and/or unnecessary burdens such as excessive meetings and special duties. See *Organizational Climate Description Questionnaire*.

homebound pupil A student capable of receiving instruction but unable to attend school. Special instruction is offered in the student's home by a visiting teacher, sometimes augmented by telephone communication between student and classroom.

homogeneous grouping The practice of assigning students to groups or classes on the basis of some likeness, usually ability. See *ability grouping* and *heterogeneous grouping*.

homeostasis Biological concept that some have applied to organizational theory. Refers to the self-regulating property inherent in living things that works to maintain normalcy within an organism. When disequilibrium of any sort (e.g., hunger) occurs, inner drives operate to bring the condition back to a normal state.

horizontal articulation The coordination of activities and/or programs at a particular level. In schools, a series of curriculum meetings involving all eighth grade teachers and other professionals serving eighth graders is an example of horizontal articulation. See *articulation* and *vertical articulation*.

horizontal organization The process of assigning a given student population to teachers for instructional purposes. Example: organizing 100 sixth graders into four self-contained classes and assigning them to each of four different teachers. See *vertical organization*.

human relations A management practice that: (1) emphasizes establishment of satisfactory interpersonal relationships with and among employees; (2) reflects the belief that the extent to which employees are involved in the decision-making process is related to morale and productivity; and (3) stresses the importance of supportive leadership.

human skill One of three basic administrative skills (the others being "conceptual skill" and "technical skill"). Human skill refers to one's ability to interact effectively with others, either individually or in groups. See *conceptual skill* and *technical skill*.

humanistic theories Theories propounded by those who believe that the major function of leadership is to create a climate in which the creative potential of organizational members can be released. Organizational members, it is held, are already personally motivated; releasing their potential will prove satisfying to them and concurrently facilitate realization of organizational goals.

hygiene factors See *motivation-hygiene theory*.

I

IDEA The Institute for Development of Educational Activities, an affiliate of the Charles F. Kettering Foundation. Organized in 1965, it works to promote change in elementary and secondary schools.

ideal-real conformity The extent to which actual role behavior conforms with ideal (expected) behavior.

idiographic leadership style One of three ("idiographic," "nomothetic," "transactional") leadership style descriptions developed by Egon Guba and Jacob Getzels. The idiographic leader is sensitive to the needs and feelings of subordinates; believes that organizational members are the most productive when working in a wholesome human relations environment. The plans and suggestions of individuals are respected. See *nomothetic leadership style* and *transactional leadership style*.

IEP See *Individualized Education Program*.

impact program Input or effort based upon expressed needs and designed to produce change.

impacted area legislation Federal laws that provide aid to local school districts experiencing sudden enrollment increases as the result of nearby military installations or defense plants. Early law was the Lanham Act, succeeded by Public Laws 815 and 874, the latter sometimes referred to as impact aid laws.

impasse Deadlock in the negotiating process between an employee organization and the employer. The bargaining process breaks down at this point, frequently resulting in the introduction of impasse resolution procedures such as mediation, fact finding, binding arbitration, or strike.

implied contract A real contract that is not expressed. Thus, the nature of the contract is inferred (frequently by the courts) from the circumstances or the behavior of the parties involved. See *express contract*.

imprest system System for handling disbursements. A fixed amount of money is set aside for some particular purpose (e.g., petty cash). Monies expended are replenished periodically to restore the fund to its original amount. Receipts or some written record of disbursements are submitted as new monies are received.

imputed negligence Negligence ascribed to an individual vicariously even though he/she did not contribute directly to the injury. For example, an employer may be held responsible for the actions of an employee; or, the owner of a vehicle may be held liable for the actions of a driver other than him/herself.

in loco parentis In Latin, means "in place of the parent." A legal doctrine which holds that when children are under the jurisdiction of the school, their teachers stand "in loco parentis" (i.e., have the right to stand in the place of the parent with respect to the children's supervision, care, and discipline).

inbasket training Method of helping administrators and administrators-to-be to analyze and resolve organizational problems. Written problems simulating reality are presented to the participant in the form of inbasket items (i.e., memos, letters, telephone messages typically found in the practicing administrator's inbasket).

incentive In management, monetary or psychological reward designed to stimulate employees to work toward optimal achievement of institutional goals.

income tax Graduated tax levied on net income; a type of progressive tax. The federal government, most states, and some local governments impose taxes on income earned by individuals and businesses. See *progressive tax*.

incompatible offices The holding of two concurrent positions that do, or are likely to, conflict with each other. Illustrating this is the teacher in a school district who seeks election/appointment to that same district's board of education.

incomplete high school Or truncated high school, a secondary school that does not offer all four years of work beyond grade 8. Applies to school systems that define grades K–8, or Pre K–8, as elementary grades.

increment See *salary increment*.

incremental budgeting A budgeting process in which annual increments (increases) are added to the preceding year's appropriations. Alternatives to this approach are PPBS and zero-base budgeting. See *decremental budgeting, planning-programming-budgeting system,* and *zero-base budgeting*.

indemnity In insurance, compensation for a sustained loss. Such compensation is normally limited to the dollar value of the insurance policy.

independent school district See *fiscally independent school district*.

independent schools Private schools; educational institutions supported by tuition, contributions, and other nonpublic revenue sources; typically governed by self-perpetuating boards of trustees.

independent study Exercises or assignments that a student completes individually and without constant supervision by a teacher.

indexed salary schedule Or ratio schedule, professional pay scale that uses the single salary schedule for teachers as a base with increments, expressed as percentages, added for experience (e.g., 3%-per-year) or for administrative responsibilities (e.g., 150% of base for service as an elementary school principal, 200% for the senior high school principalship).

indifferents One of three classes of employees who exhibit certain common behaviors relating to ambition. According to Robert Presthus, creator of the term, indifferents: (1) are satisfied to perform at only minimal levels; (2) prefer to stay out of the limelight; (3) tend not to identify closely with the organization; (4) usually derive their satisfaction from sources other than their jobs; and (5) tend to see their jobs as mere instruments to obtain off-work satisfactions. See *ambivalents* and *upward mobiles*.

indirect costs Or overhead costs, necessary costs that cannot be associated accurately or readily with a specific program, unit, service or activity. Examples include expenditures for utilities, basic supplies, supervision, and rent.

Individualized Education Program (IEP) Written instructional plan for each handicapped child, required by Public Law 94-142 and to be developed by a team that includes the child's parents/guardians. IEP's include: (1) a description of the child's performance; (2) instructional (annual) goals; (3) resources/services to be provided; (4) dates covered by the program; and (5) criteria to be used to determine if objectives have been met.

individually prescribed instruction (IPI) A form of individualized instruction based on sequenced instructional objectives. Objectives are developed for individual subjects (e.g., mathematics) and stated behaviorally. Diagnostic tests determine each student's placement in the sequence and the prescribed activities he/she is to perform.

induction, employee See *orientation*.

infant school In the United Kingdom and several Commonwealth countries, a public school for young children (ages 5–7 or 8); frequently referred to as British Infant School.

influence The capacity to induce behavioral changes in individuals or groups. In formal organizations, influence is multi-directional (i.e., hierarchically, it may be exerted upward, downward, or laterally).

informal communication In organizations, an unofficial system of communication in which people communicate with other people without regard to the office or status of the individuals involved (frequently on a social basis). The "grapevine" is one example of informal communication. See *communication, formal communication*, and *grapevine*.

informal group Unofficial system of interpersonal relationships within a formal organization in which there is a shared feeling of concern. Such groups frequently influence decision-making within the formal organization.

informal organization System of relationships within a formal organization that: (1) are not officially recognized, (2) consist of small groups of compatible persons who (3) discuss job-related and non-job related subjects. Informal organizations can perform several important functions: (1) affect decision-making; (2) facilitate communication (e.g., grapevine); (3) influence morale; (4) provide feedback; and (5) facilitate or block goal realization. Research indicates that these "structures" are sometimes permanent; their activities may or may not be compatible with those of the formal organization.

information processing See *data processing*.

information retrieval A procedure in which information is recovered from stored data.

initial demand In collective bargaining, the first statement (position) presented by representatives of the bargaining unit. The agreement finally reached normally represents a scaling down of this first in a round of requests. See *initial offer*.

initial offer In collective bargaining, the first response (statement) made by management to the employee organization's initial demand. See *initial demand*.

initiating structure One of two leader behavior dimensions measured by the Leader Behavior Description Questionnaire (LBDQ). Factors comprising "initiating structure" are those which: (1) delineate the relationship between leader and group members, and (2) establish well-defined patterns of organization, communication channels, and operating procedures. Emphasis is on *organizing, goal definition,* and *directing work*. The second LBDQ dimension is "consideration." See *consideration* and *Leader Behavior Description Questionnaire*.

initiative In some states, a procedure that permits the people, through petition, to propose new laws or constitutional amendments. In contrast to the referendum, a reactive procedure, the initiative is proactive insofar as the people are concerned. See *referendum*.

injunction Or labor injunction, a court order that restrains individuals or groups (e.g., unions, employers) from performing acts that are apt to result in injury to property, to the rights of others, or to the rights of the community. Orders imposed before a formal hearing is conducted are known as "temporary restraining orders"; "permanent injunctions" are issued following such a hearing.

inner city school School that (1) is located in a densely populated, usually poor, urban area, and (2) enrolls a relatively large ratio of educationally disadvantaged students.

innovation A novel change that is adopted and supported because it is considered to be a practical advance in accomplishing the goals of a system.

input Introduction or insertion of information. In data processing, information that is fed into the internal storage unit of a computer.

inputs-outputs Terms used in connection with the systems approach. "Inputs" comprise the several resources available to help an organization reach its goals (e.g., money, material, talent); "outputs" are the ends (resultants) actually achieved. See *output*.

inservice education Program of planned activities for incumbent employees designed to improve their on-the-job performance. Inservice programs in education are normally sponsored to bring about instructional improvement by: (1) expanding teachers' knowledge; (2) improving individual teacher effectiveness; and (3) encouraging teachers to want to improve themselves.

institutional self-study A written analysis of a school's (or school system's) strengths and weaknesses prepared by the institution seeking accreditation or reaccreditation of its programs. Institutional self-studies are prepared in accordance with guidelines formulated by the accrediting agency.

instruction Activities dealing with the teaching of one or more learners.

instructional materials center (IMC) Also known as an instructional media center or learning resource center, the instructional space in a school in which library and audio-visual services are provided. Includes print materials, software, equipment, reading/listening/viewing areas, and production areas.

instructional supervision Supervisory activities and practices related to the improvement of instruction (e.g., clinical supervision, conferencing, materials development) as distinguished from noninstructional supervisory activities such as cafeteria services, census, and transportation.

insubordination Refusal to submit to constituted authority of a superior.

intangible asset See *fixed asset*.

integrated day Or unstructured day, in open education, the large blocks of time during which children pursue individual activities.

integration, racial A sequel to school desegregation, achieved when comfortable social interaction among students of all races and all ethnic backgrounds becomes reality. See *desegregation* and *racial balance*.

intelligence quotient (I.Q.) Or ratio I.Q., a measure of brightness or rate of mental development; compares an individual's mental age (MA) to his/her chronological age (CA); more specifically, MA/CA × 100. In recent years, the deviation I.Q. has begun to replace this measure. See *deviation I.Q.*

interaction analysis Observation system for gathering data based on verbal communication (interaction) in a classroom. Focus is on the teaching-learning process. Most systems involve trained observers who collect and categorize data that are subsequently analyzed for research/training/supervision purposes.

interaction-expectation theories Leadership theories which focus on the *interactions* and behavioral *expectations* members of an organization have for each member. According to these theories, successful leaders are those who demonstrate ability to initiate and maintain role structures.

interfund In accounting, the act of transferring money from one account and adding it to another.

interim borrowing Short-term loans taken out by a board of education, usually in anticipation of income from taxes or proceeds from the issuance of a bond. See *bond anticipation note*.

intermediate level Grades immediately above the primary level; usually grades 4, 5, and 6.

intermediate unit Also known as intermediate administrative unit or intermediate school district, a "between" unit operating below the state level and above the school district level. In some states, it is a regulatory arm of the state, overseeing an assigned region; in others, it is a confederation of school districts organized to provide specialized services that no member district is able to provide alone.

internship Or administration internship, an extended field experience during which trainees are helped to see the relationship between theory and practice in educational administration. Interns are normally assigned to work under the direction of practicing administrators, are supervised by university faculty members, and participate in decision-making activities within the system or school to which they have been assigned. See *cooperating administrator*.

inter-role conflict Situation that arises when an employee works with individuals or groups whose differing expectations of him/her are incompatible. See *intra-role conflict*.

interstate migratory child A child who, in the company of parent or guardian, has moved across state lines within the last twelve months, and such move: (1) was made in order that a parent/guardian/family member might secure temporary (or seasonal) agricultural or agriculture-related employment, and (2) is expected to recur as the family continues to migrate. See *intrastate migratory child*.

intervening variable An unplanned factor/input whose introduction influences or modifies a process.

intervention Specific and planned action by a change agent undertaken to interrupt status quo and to foster change.

interventionist See *change agent*.

intimacy One of four teacher behavior dimensions (subtests) included in the OCDQ. The term is applied to teachers who enjoy close and friendly relations with their peers. See *Organizational Climate Description Questionnaire*.

intra-role conflict Problem that arises when an individual fulfills two concurrent roles (e.g., father and principal) and the expectations of one conflict with those of the other. See *inter-role conflict*.

intrastate migratory child A child who, in the company of parent or guardian, has moved across school boundaries within a state within the last twelve months, and such move: (1) was made in order that a parent/guardian/family member might secure temporary (or seasonal) agricultural or agriculture-related employment, and (2) is expected to recur as the family continues to migrate. See *interstate migratory child*.

intrinsic motivation See *motivation*.

inventory A detailed list or record indicating all articles (supplies and equipment) on hand. For each article recorded, the typical inventory includes/shows: (1) quantity on hand; (2) article description; and (3) unit value.

invoice An itemized list of materials purchased from a single vendor. The list normally includes basic information for each article such as unit price, description, quantity, date of purchase, and terms.

I.Q. See *intelligence quotient.*

issue In labor relations, an item for negotiation; may be initiated by either the employer or the employee organization.

itinerant teacher A traveling teacher; one who works in more than one school for the purpose of: (1) working directly with children who have special needs, and (2) providing individual advice/assistance to regular teachers.

J–K

Jarvis-Gann Property-Tax Incentive See *Proposition 13*.

job analysis The process of studying organizational positions for the purpose of ascertaining factors such as job-holder's duties, training required, rate of pay, working hours, and relationships with other positions; sometimes referred to as a job examination or job study. The process is often carried out prior to the preparation of a job description. See *job description*.

job classification Or job grading, the grouping of jobs into specific classes, levels, or categories. Factors used to differentiate one classification from another include skill, experience, nature and extent of training, and knowledge. Jobs within a given classification usually have similar rates of pay.

job description A broad statement or outline that indicates the scope, qualifications, position relationships, and principal duties of a particular job. Job descriptions are management tools commonly used when recruiting, selecting, training, evaluating, and rewarding job holders.

job enlargement The adding of tasks or operations to be performed by an employee without changing his/her status, compensation, or opportunity for upward mobility; not to be confused with job enrichment. See *job enrichment*.

job enrichment Upgrading or expanding a position, usually in one or more of the following ways: (1) expanding work content; (2) increasing challenge; (3) increasing the position's status; (4) increasing the level of responsibility; or (5) providing greater autonomy. Enrichment makes work more meaningful for the employee and facilitates his/her upward mobility in the organization.

job examination See *job analysis.*

job posting Method of announcing job vacancies by placing notices of job openings in centrally-located areas. Such notices usually indicate basic information such as job qualifications, duties, method of applying, and deadline date for filing.

job satisfaction The degree to which an employee's job fulfills his/her personal/professional needs and accords with his/her values.

job sheet See *time sheet.*

job specification A listing of the skills, abilities, characteristics, and knowledge necessary for successful implementation of a particular job description. See *job description.*

job study See *job analysis.*

Johari Window Model, developed by Joseph Luft and Harry Ingham, used to gain greater insight into one's own behavior. Consists of a square divided into four quadrants: (1) the public self; (2) the blind self; (3) the private self; and (4) the unknown area.

joint bargaining Process in which two or more unions, working in tandem, negotiate an agreement with their common employer.

Joplin Plan A system of organization in which elementary school children, regardless of age or grade level, are grouped homogeneously according to reading achievement. Reading instruction is then offered on a whole-class basis. The system, frequently used in the intermediate grades, was introduced in the Joplin, Missouri school district (1952).

journal (1) Business administration term for any book of original entry; the book in which transactions are recorded before being posted in a ledger. (2) Professional magazine/periodical.

jurisdiction Authority granted by law.

jurisdictional dispute Controversy between two or more employee organizations. Such disputes usually revolve around one of two questions: (1) Which unit shall represent a particular group of employees for collective bargaining purposes? or (2) Which of two or more existing units' members shall perform a certain type of work?

just cause Basis for terminating the services of an employee. In education, just cause is normally used to mean incompetence and/or misconduct.

juvenile delinquent Child or youth who violates the law or persistently exhibits anti-social behavior. Specific legal definitions vary from one state to another.

Keogh Plan Or Keogh Act Plan, retirement plan for self-employed individuals (e.g., doctors, lawyers). Authorized by the Self-Employed Individuals Tax Retirement Act; contains certain tax advantages.

key results analysis Study of an administrator's job for the purpose of identifying and analyzing (sometimes quantifying) the key tasks contributing to job success.

keypunch (1) Or card punch, machine with a keyboard that punches holes in a card to represent data (noun). (2) To cut holes into a punch card, using a coding system, for subsequent data processing or computer use (verb).

L

labor injunction See *injunction*.

laboratory school A school operating under the supervision of a teacher training institution. Used by schools/colleges of education for: (1) demonstration teaching; (2) student teaching; and/or (3) research. An early laboratory school was established in 1896, at the University of Chicago, by John Dewey.

laissez-faire leadership One of three commonly recognized types of leadership ("democratic" vs. "laissez-faire" vs. "autocratic") identified by Kurt Lewin and his colleagues (1939). The laissez-faire leader tends to be a "do nothing" individual; is neither democratic nor autocratic; may respond to group inquiries, but is disinclined to intervene in the affairs of the organization; and, does little planning for or with the group. See *autocratic leadership* and *democratic leadership*.

Lancastrian system Educational structure developed by the Englishman, Joseph Lancaster, and subsequently adopted by New York City in the early 1800's. Using the system, one schoolmaster taught a dozen or so of his brightest students; these pupils, called monitors, were then responsible for instructing other students. One schoolmaster was thus able to "teach" 200–600 children, and at little cost.

language (1) System for communicating information based on a set of representations, conventions, and rules. May involve transmission/reception of information between people or between people and machines. (2) In data processing, a computer language (e.g., BASIC, Cobol, Fortran).

latent functions The consequences of a policy or program that were not intended. See *manifest functions*.

Latin grammar school An early secondary school that prepared male students for university study; forerunner to the public comprehensive high school. Its curriculum stressed study of the classics. The Boston Latin Grammar School, founded in 1635, was one of the earliest and best known of such schools.

law of effect A motivational concept, formulated by Edward L. Thorndike, stating that behavior followed by a positive (i.e., pleasurable) consequence will tend to recur. Conversely, behavior followed by a negative consequence will tend not to recur.

LBDQ See *Leader Behavior Description Questionnaire.*

leader An individual chosen or appointed to lead a group and to influence its activities toward realization of the group's goals; the directing head of a group.

leader behavior Behavior exhibited by a leader while working with others in a formal organization. Students of leader behavior give particular attention to the nature and degree of influence being exercised.

Leader Behavior Description Questionnaire (LBDQ) Instrument, developed by John K. Hemphill and Alvin E. Coons, that assesses leader behavior. Two dimensions of leadership are tested: (1) "consideration," and (2) "initiating structure." See *consideration* and *initiating structure.*

leadership The proactive integration of an organization's people, materials, and ideas such that activities and efforts are directed toward realization of institutional goals. The willingness of an organization's members to be led is regarded by many as a function of the leader's personal qualities.

learning Knowledge acquired or changed behavior resulting from study, practice, and/or experience.

learning curve Or skill acquisition curve, a graph showing rate of learning, or task improvement, by an individual or a group. Two variables are depicted: elapsed time and progress.

learning disabled Individuals who exhibit a marked difference between expected achievement and actual poor achievement. Discrepancies usually reflect poor ability to use/understand language.

Conditions such as brain injury, dyslexia, perceptual handicaps, and minimal brain dysfunction fall within the definition.

learning resource center See *instructional materials center*.

learning theory Logical framework for the systematic presentation and study of facts related to learning processes. Classical theory groupings include: (1) S-R theories; (2) classical conditioning; (3) operative conditioning; and (4) cognitive learning.

lease Contract between a property owner and a lessee (e.g., tenant) that grants the lessee use of a particular property, for a stipulated period of time, in exchange for a fixed rental fee.

least restrictive environment A concept, grounded in law, requiring that handicapped individuals receive an education as comparable as feasible to that being received by their nonhandicapped peers. The idea of mainstreaming emerged out of this concept. See *mainstreaming*.

least squares technique A personnel administration procedure for establishing rates of pay (i.e., a wage structure) for different jobs. A statistical formula is used to grade different positions; wage ranges for each grade are then established.

leave Legitimate absence of an employee from duty assignment. Such absence does not affect his/her employment status.

leave, annual See *annual leave*.

leave, maternity See *maternity leave*.

leave, military See *military leave*.

leave of absence An extended absence from work for which the employee is usually not paid. Shorter leaves of this type are referred to as leaves without pay. See *leave without pay*.

leave, personal See *personal leave*.

leave, sabbatical See *sabbatical leave*.

leave, sick See *sick leave*.

leave without pay Relatively short absence from work; a nonpay status normally granted at the employee's request. Longer leaves of this type are known as leaves of absence. See *leave of absence*.

ledger Individual accounts in which the financial transactions of a fund are recorded. Examples of such accounts include Income Accounts, Expenditure Accounts, and Cash at Bank accounts.

legitimate power Or formal authority, official power which is accorded to an individual by law, by mandate of an official body (such as a school board), or by a superordinate. Legitimate power is one of five power classifications developed by John R.P. French, Jr. and Bertram Raven. See *coercive power, expert power, referent power,* and *reward power*.

lesson plan Written plan for a lesson to be taught during a single class period. Such plans normally include entries identifying objectives, review items, new material, points to be stressed, reference materials, and assignments to be made.

levy (1) To impose taxes or special assessments (verb). (2) The total of taxes or special assessments imposed by a governmental unit (e.g., total taxes imposed on a school district to support the operation of its schools for a specified period of time) (noun).

liability (1) Debt owed by an individual or an institution, and payable in goods or services. (2) In accounting, *liabilities* (pl) mean the credit half of a balance sheet. (3) In law, the state of being liable.

libel A defamation that is written; published statement that: (1) is false and malicious, and (2) injures an individual's reputation. See *slander*.

library books Volumes available for use by all, not just certain students (e.g., those in a particular grade level). Included are dictionaries and other reference works; excluded are periodicals and textbooks.

lifelong learning The acquisition of knowledge throughout adulthood. Learning may be formal or informal; fulfills vocational, professional, personal, and/or recreational needs.

lighthouse school/school system A school or school system that is recognized as a leader in educational innovation; a pioneering institution sometimes referred to as being "on the growing edge."

Likert method Procedure for measuring attitudes, named for its developer, Rensis Likert. Written statements are presented to which the individual responds, agreeing or disagreeing. Typical Likert scale consists of five possible responses examples of which are: SA (strongly agree), A (agree), U (undecided), D (disagree), and SD (strongly disagree).

line relationship The relationship among positions in an organizational hierarchy which clearly designates decision-making and accountability dimensions. See *staff relationship*.

line and staff organization In formal organizations, the dividing of administrative roles into line or staff categories. Line officers (e.g., superintendents, principals) have decision-making authority and authority over subordinates; staff officers (e.g., counselors, librarians), as specialists, provide resource assistance or advice.

linear programming One of several quantitative approaches to decision-making. This approach helps the administrator to determine minimal or optimal alternatives to the solving of a problem when: (1) several variables exist, and (2) these are related linearly (i.e., they have straight-line relationships).

line-item budget See *budget, line-item*.

linker One who disseminates; more specifically, an intermediary who serves as a communication bridge between those who originate knowledge and those who use it. In agriculture, for example, the county agent serves as linker between university scientists and farmers.

litigant A party to a lawsuit.

local basic administrative unit Synonym for "school district" or "local education agency."

local education agency (LEA) A legislative term applied to a local level agency that operates public schools or contracts for educational services; usually a school district.

locals Workers in an organization who, according to Alvin W. Gouldner, are: (1) high on loyalty to their employing organization; (2) low on commitment to their specialization or professional skills; and (3) likely to identify with an inner reference group. Gouldner identified four *local* types: the "dedicated," the "true bureaucrats," the "homeguard," and the "elders." See *cosmopolitans*.

lockout Action taken by an employer in which employees are refused access to their place of employment, thus preventing them from performing their work. The opposite of a strike, the lockout is resorted to for the purpose of applying pressure on employees, usually with the hope of influencing the resolution of a labor dispute.

loop A series of instructions to a computer that cause some part of a program to be repeated (executed) until a predetermined terminal objective is achieved.

lower division In colleges and universities, the first two (i.e., freshman and sophomore) years of a baccalaureate program. See *upper division*.

lowerarchy Workers in an organization who hold middle or bottom level positions.

loyalty oath Affirmation of allegiance to the U.S. Constitution, sometimes to a state constitution as well. The U.S. Supreme Court has approved use of oaths requiring an employee to disavow intent to overthrow the government, but has rejected oaths that vaguely define subversive activities. Additionally, teachers may not be dismissed for being members of an organization considered to be subversive.

M

magnet school Alternative school whose distinctive programs and resources are intended to attract, voluntarily, students from all segments of the community and from all racial-ethnic groups. Such schools usually feature curriculum specialties (e.g., the arts, sciences, vocational education).

mainstreaming The practice of assigning handicapped students to classes of nonhandicapped students. Its purpose is to permit them to have maximum contact with the nonhandicapped. The school provides individual handicapped students with needed support personnel and services.

maintenance of plant Funds spent on salaries and supplies for the purpose of repairing or replacing school buildings, grounds, and equipment.

maintenance synergy See *synergy*.

major medical benefit Type of health insurance that protects against catastrophic medical expenses. Benefits above a certain amount (high deductible) are paid upon claim.

malfeasance The commission of a wrongful or illegal act by an official in office.

malpractice Improper professional conduct, willful or non-willful; a serious breach of a professional code or duty.

malpractice insurance Insurance that covers the policyholder against charges of professional misconduct or lack of ordinary skill in carrying out a professional act. Such insurance is available to educators.

management The effort or activity necessary to direct a particular task or a total enterprise. More particularly, the individual(s) who work with and through people, who administer(s) facilities, funds, materials, and other resources to achieve organizational goals.

management by objectives A term, first used by Peter F. Drucker (*Practice by Management,* 1954), used to describe a collaborative and ongoing planning procedure involving managers and their superiors. The procedure consists of several steps: (1) establishment of measurable goals; (2) listing of procedures to achieve the goals; and (3) performance evaluation, with the originally stated goals serving as criteria. Goals are modified if the evaluation suggests the need for such change.

management information system (MIS) Systematic data-gathering method for acquiring, retrieving, and redistributing data for the purpose of aiding management with decision-making. Information provided is both organized and current.

management prerogatives The administrative rights implicitly or explicitly reserved for management in a collective bargaining agreement.

management team See *team administration*.

managerial grid Two-dimensional training device, developed by Robert Blake and Jane Mouton, consisting of a grid with two conceptual axes: (1) "concern for people" and (2) "concern for production." One is vertical, the other horizontal. Each axis is scaled, 1–9. Responses to stimulus problems are plotted, one score for each of the two dimensions. Management styles are inferred from score patterns.

mandamus A writ, issued by a superior court and directed to an inferior court, corporation, or official, which demands the performance of a legally required duty or public act.

mandatory four-quarter plan See *four-quarter plan*.

mandatory legislation Laws that all school districts must follow. See *permissive legislation*.

manifest functions The consequences of a policy or program that were intended and realized. See *latent functions*.

market value See *true value*.

marking system Method employed by a school or school system for reporting pupil progress. Most commonly employed systems mark students using "ABCDEF," "percentages," "pass-fail," and "satisfactory-unsatisfactory."

Maslow's theory See *hierarchy-of-needs theory*.

mastery learning Theory formulated by Benjamin Bloom which holds that all children are capable of understanding a concept appropriate to their age. It presumes that curriculum is correctly structured and instruction is effective; acknowledges that learning rates will vary from individual to individual.

maternity leave An officially approved absence from work granted to female employees for childbirth. Time off before and following the birth of a child is usually allowed.

matriculation The formal acceptance and registration of a student into an educational institution. (Generally used in the context of higher education.)

matrix Rectangular (two-dimensional) arrangement of numbers and terms placed into rows and columns; used to study relationships.

maximization In decision-making, selection of the best of all alternatives/options available.

MBO See *management by objectives*.

mean The arithmetic average. Expressed as a formula:

$$\text{Mean} = \frac{\text{Sum of all scores}}{\text{No. of scores}}.$$

median A statistical measure of central tendency. The middle score (item) in a distribution of scores that has been arranged in order of magnitude (i.e., high to low, or vice-versa); the score above and below which half of all scores lie. In the following distribution of numbers, each representing a child's weight, 78 is the median number (weight): 87, 84, 84, 78, 76, 73, 70.

mediated instruction Instruction carried out using media (e.g., film, television, recording, radio) rather than the traditional face-to-face interaction between teacher and learner(s).

mediation Efforts by a neutral third party to help resolve disputes between employers and employees. Mediators engage in fact-finding, make interpretations, and offer advice. Their recommendations are almost always nonbinding.

membership The number of students officially registered (or "belonging") in a school or school system on a particular day. Includes students absent as well as those who are present. See *average daily membership*.

mental age (M.A.) Score on a test of mental ability expressed in terms of chronological age. MA is that age for which an individual's score is average. For example, a pupil whose mental ability test score is equal to the average score earned by children who are 7½ years old is said to have an MA of 7.5.

mentally retarded Category of exceptional students with: (1) significantly subaverage general intellectual functioning (some define this operationally as an I.Q. of 70 or less), and (2) concurrent problems of an adaptive behavior nature. Both characteristics are manifested during the developmental period.

merit pay Extra salary awarded to employees in recognition of outstanding job performance.

merit rating A personnel evaluation system that relates compensation to quality of employee performance. In teaching, rewards for outstanding performance can take the form of additional salary increments; for poor performers, normally scheduled increments may be withheld. Two problems frequently encountered in connection with merit rating of teachers relate to: (1) the defining and measuring of meritorious teaching, and (2) insuring rater objectivity.

microteaching Preservice and inservice teacher training technique, developed at Stanford University, that focuses on specific teaching skills. A brief lesson is taught by the trainee; videotaped; critiqued by the trainee, fellow trainees, or supervisor; and then repeated. The class is scaled down in terms of size (5–6 pupils) and time (5–12 minutes). The technique is calculated to give the trainee a measure of success in teaching and immediate feedback.

middle school Separately administered school whose students are predominantly pre-adolescents. The middle school includes pre-high school grade levels, usually 5–8 or 6–8, and offers a transitional program between elementary education and secondary education.

migrant child See *interstate migratory child* and *intrastate migratory child*.

migrant education Program of instruction and related services provided to children of temporary (or seasonal) agricultural workers whose families move frequently across school boundaries or state lines. See *interstate migratory child* and *intrastate migratory child*.

military leave Leave, without loss of tenure, that is allowed an employee while in the armed forces (drafted or engaged in military reserve training). Such leave: (1) is mandatory providing the teacher or administrator has been employed for more than half a year; (2) does not entitle the employee to his/her regular salary while on leave; and (3) guarantees, within certain time limits, that the returning employee may return to his/her original position.

minicourse A short course, one that can be completed in a few days or weeks.

minimum competency testing A testing program, state or locally mandated, which seeks to measure specific competencies and/or skills in relation to a defined standard. Tests are of the paper-and pencil variety. Their results may be used: (1) to determine eligibility for promotion or graduation; (2) to evaluate a school or school system; (3) to classify students for assignment purposes; or (4) to allocate funds (often for remedial purposes).

minimum competency testing A type of evaluation that measures the acquisition of a competency or skill using a predetermined and specified standard. Such tests are used in some schools to test for basic skill mastery, in others to determine students' eligibility for promotion or graduation.

ministerial duty An official duty that provides the administrator no room for the exercise of discretion; an absolute duty. Such duty contrasts with discretionary duty. See *discretionary duty*.

minority For Equal Employment Opportunity purposes, this term includes blacks, American Indians, orientals, and persons with Spanish surnames; a term commonly used to describe persons not of the majority population with respect to race, color, religion, or ethnic background.

minute book Official (and frequently required) record of proceedings containing a description of all actions taken by the board of education during its meetings.

misfeasance Improper performance of a lawful act.

mixed grouping See *heterogeneous grouping*.

mobility aid Cane, seeing eye dog, electronic device, or other device that helps blind people to move about.

mock rules One of three types of organizational rules identified by Alvin Gouldner. Mock rules are neither obeyed by employees nor enforced by management. Neither group identifies with such rules; hence, their violation engenders little or no anxiety. Example of a mock rule: the "no eating" sign in a college classroom that everyone ignores. See *representative rules* and *punishment-centered rules*.

modal grade The grade level in which most pupils of a particular chronological age are enrolled.

mode In a distribution of scores or other numbers, the item that occurs most frequently; a measure of central tendency.

model Representation, simulation, or abstracted intellectual pattern that: (1) describes data using a system of symbols, and (2) may be used to study trends and various interrelationships.

modeling Teaching by exhibition. A training procedure in which trainees (e.g., student teachers, administrative interns) learn appropriate role behaviors by observing selected role models (e.g., critic teachers, cooperating administrators) at work. Accurate perception, recall, and synthesis on the part of the learner are required. May be carried out "live" or by videotape.

modular schedule A school schedule made up of relatively short time modules usually ranging from 5–30 minutes in length. Classes meet for different lengths of time during the week. For example, in a high school using 10 minute modules, a science class may meet for three modules (30 minutes) on Monday, five modules on Tuesday, and twelve modules (for a laboratory) on Thursday of a given week. See *flexible schedule*.

module (1) Shortest unit of time (e.g., five minutes) used for scheduling purposes. (2) In data processing, an identifiable unit of hardware or software that is used with other units.

monitorial school See *Lancastrian system*.

Montessori method Instructional method for educating preschool children, developed by the Italian physician, Dr. Maria Montessori. Internationally popular, the method stresses sensory-motor learning using special materials and is taught by teachers trained especially in the Montessori method.

moral turpitude A base or vile act that is contrary to justice, honesty, modesty, or good morals; may be used as grounds for termination of tenured teachers.

morale An employee's attitude toward his/her job and work environment (including peers, supervisors, facilities, and resources). See *esprit*.

motivation Inner drive that moves or activates an individual; includes incentives or inducements such as goals, dreams, desires, and wishes. "Intrinsic motivation" results from an indiviual's personal need/desire to perform well; "extrinsic motivation" refers to behaviors motivated by factors that are external to the individual.

motivation-hygiene theory Management theory, advanced by Frederick Herzberg, that deals with subordinate motivation. Two sets of factors are identified: (1) hygiene factors, or "dissatisfiers," environmental factors that contribute to job dissatisfaction, and (2) motivations, or "satisfiers," those factors that have a motivational thrust and contribute to growth. See *dissatisfiers* and *satisfiers*.

motivators See *motivation-hygiene theory*.

movable equipment An item of equipment that is transportable. Relocation of such equipment neither damages it nor devalues/alters the location from which it is taken.

multidisciplinary staffing team The various educational professionals and the parent who collectively: (1) identify the needs of the exceptional child; (2) formulate an individualized program for him/her; and (3) determine his/her appropriate placement. See *staffing*.

multigrading Organizational plan for cross-grading in elementary schools. Groups of students from two or three sequential grade levels (e.g., 4–5, 2–3–4) are deliberately assigned to one teacher. An intermediate step between grading and nongrading.

multihandicapped Category of exceptional students with more than one physical or mental impairment (e.g., mentally retarded-blind). The combination is so severe that the student can not be accommodated in special education classes established solely for one of the impairments.

municipal bond A bond issued by a state, county, city, town, village, or a state agency/authority.

municipal overburden In large cities, the noneducation services (e.g., welfare, sanitation) that must be provided and with which education competes for funding.

mutual insurance company An insurance company owned by the policyholders. Such companies have no stock; company profits are distributed among the policyholders. See *stock insurance company*.

N

NAEP See *National Assessment of Educational Progress.*

NAESP See *National Association of Elementary School Principals.*

NASSP See *National Association of Secondary School Principals.*

National Academy for School Executives (NASE) The inservice arm of the American Association for School Administrators. Seminars and workshops are conducted in various parts of the country under the auspices of NASE's 15-member Board of Directors. See *American Association of School Administrators.*

National Assessment of Educational Progress (NAEP) Federally-supported project that selects large samples of American students and tests their performance in selected subject fields and on the basis of specific objectives. From 1964 to 1983 NAEP has been carried out by the Education Commission of the States.

National Association of Elementary School Principals (NAESP) Founded in 1921 as a department of the National Education Association, presently an autonomous organization for elementary school administrators. NAESP publishes *Principal* (formerly *National Elementary Principal*), a journal.

National Association of Independent Schools (NAIS) National organization of nonprofit, nondiscriminatory, and regionally-accredited independent schools that have been in operation for at least five years. Membership is institutional. NAIS was organized in 1962.

National Association of Secondary School Principals (NASSP) An independent national organization of secondary school principals, assistant secondary school principals, and others interested in secondary school administration. Founded in 1916; sponsors the National Honor Society and the Junior Honor Society. NASSP was formerly a department of the National Education Association. Publications include the *NASSP Bulletin,* a journal.

National Conference of Professors of Educational Administration (NCPEA) Official name for an annual conference of professors of educational administration. Created in 1947, NCPEA has no headquarters or full-time staff. Extended work-sessions are held each August with a different university hosting each conference.

National Council for Accreditation of Teacher Education An organization accrediting higher education programs that prepare teachers and other professional school personnel. It is the only teacher education accreditation body recognized by the U.S. Secretary of Education.

National Education Association (NEA) Largest national organization of teachers in the world. First organized in 1857 as the National Teachers' Association; boasts 1.8 million members. NEA publishes *Today's Education, NEA Reporter,* as well as numbers of special reports and research bulletins.

National Honor Society (NHS) Organization, sponsored by the National Association of Secondary School Principals, that recognizes academically outstanding secondary school students. Membership is by election and limited to students with a gpa of 85%, a B average, or its equivalent.

National School Boards Association (NSBA) The national organization of school boards (state/territorial school boards and local boards of education). Organized in 1940 as the National Council of State School Boards Association, NSBA assumed its present name in 1948. Publications include *The American School Board Journal.*

native language The language normally used by individuals possessing limited English-speaking ability. When applied to a child, "native language" means that language normally used by his/her parents.

NCATE See *National Council for Accreditation of Teacher Education.*

NCPEA See *National Conference of Professors of Educational Administration.*

NEA See *National Education Association.*

needs assessment A systematic way to determine institutional goals. Existing programs/practices are assessed; needed programs/practices are identified. Thereafter, an active plan emerges for closing the gap between "what is" and "what is needed."

negentropy Organizational concept which holds that, in an open system, energic input needs to be greater than its output if the system is to survive. The input-output disparity is accounted for by the resources the organization requires and consumes to sustain itself.

neglected child A child who has been: (1) abandoned/neglected by his/her parents, or whose parents are deceased, and (2) in accordance with law, assigned to a residential institution for custodial supervision.

negligence The doing of that which a reasonably prudent person would not do, or the failure to do that which a reasonably prudent person would have done, in similar circumstances, to care for the safety or well-being of others. Such imprudent behavior may make one open to tort liability should it cause injury to others.

negligence, comparative See *comparative negligence.*

negligence, contributory See *contributory negligence.*

negligence, imputed See *imputed negligence.*

negotiating team Or system bargaining team, the group of officials authorized to represent the school system at the collective bargaining table; the board of education's counterpart to the union team.

negotiating unit See *bargaining unit.*

negotiation In collective bargaining, the process by which employee representatives and employers (or their representatives) bargain over employee concerns such as salaries, fringe benefits, working conditions, and grievance procedures.

neighborhood school A school located in close proximity to the homes of its students; one that serves the local community in which it is located.

nepotism In an organization, the practice of employing/rewarding one's relatives in favor of others and doing so on the basis of kinship rather than merit.

network In data processing, an interconnected system of computers and/or terminals that: (1) need not be geographically proximate to each other, and (2) are frequently connected via telephone lines.

nominal damages See *damages*.

nomothetic leadership style One of three ("nomothetic," "idiographic," "transactional") leadership style descriptions formulated by Egon Guba and Jacob Getzels. The nomothetic leader demands conformity of role behavior, effectiveness, and adherence to organizational regulations; subordinates the needs of individuals to the requirements of the organization; and uses sanctions. See *idiographic leadership style* and *transactional leadership style*.

nondirective interviewing An interview technique in which open-ended questions are posed; those being interviewed are expected to do most of the talking.

noncallable bonds A bond that cannot be "called in" (redeemed) before its specified maturity date.

noncategorical In school finance, revenues from various sources that can not be associated with any particular expenditure.

noncontributory Group insurance or pension plan in which the employer pays all premiums; opposite of contributory.

nonfeasance Failure to perform some act that should be performed; disregard or nonfulfillmment of a duty.

nonfunctional hearing See *deaf*.

nongraded school plan Also known as "ungraded school," "continuous progress plan," or "ungraded primary plan;" a plan in which some or all grade levels (usually in the elementary school) are organized in keeping with the philosophy of nongrading. See *nongrading*.

nongrading A flexible student grouping practice based on the notion of continuous progress. Grade level designations are removed, thus reducing or eliminating problems frequently associated with retention and acceleration. Individual student differences are accommodated and students progress at their own rate.

nonoperating school district A legally constituted school district that operates no schools. Such districts: (1) have governing bodies (school boards), and (2) enroll their children in a neighboring school district on a tuition basis.

nonpromotion Retaining a student in his/her present grade/course at the close of the academic term or year while most other students are advanced to the next higher level. Retainees are normally expected to repeat the grade/course in question. The major reason for nonpromotion is less than satisfactory academic performance.

nonpublic school See *independent schools* and *private school*.

nonrenewal In education, action taken to terminate a probationary teacher's employment at the close of his/her contract period; not a synonym for "dismissal." See *dismissal*.

nonresident student A student whose legal residence falls outside the boundaries of a particular school attendance area, school system, or institution.

nonserved child Handicapped student of legal school age who is not in school because the local school system offers no program that meets his/her unique needs.

nonverbal communication The intentional or unintentional process of transmitting information by way of body gestures, facial expressions, and the way in which one uses space and time. See *body language*.

norm-referenced test A test in which an individual's score/performance is compared with test results recorded by some reference group. Unlike criterion-referenced tests, which measure "what ought to be," norm-referenced tests measure "what is" (relative to one's peers). See *criterion-referenced test*.

normal capacity The number of students that can be accommodated in the instruction rooms of a school building during a school day (excluding multiple sessions). Such capacity is usually determined using state standards.

normal distribution A distribution of scores which, when plotted graphically, is said to be bell-shaped. When scores are distributed normally, they: (1) tend to cluster around the mean; (2) taper toward each extreme; and (3) are symmetrically distributed. In a normal distribution, "mean" and "median" are the same.

normal schools Teacher training schools prevalent in the United States through the nineteenth and early twentieth centuries. Most prepared students for careers as elementary school teachers.

normative power See *compliance typology*.

norms (1) Rules of behavior indicating right from wrong; standards of conduct. (2) In testing, the average scores recorded for defined groups and against which individual scores are compared.

North Denver Plan Plan, introduced into the North Denver, Colorado schools (1898) that featured enrichment and independent study opportunities for brighter pupils.

notice Official announcement of a forthcoming meeting. In general, a school board meeting is lawful only if appropriate notice has been given to individual board members. Several states require such notification for the benefit of the public as well.

notice to bidders Special bid form, distributed to possible bidders in advance of a bid opening, on which individual bidders indicate their prices for the item(s) described by the bid-soliciting agency.

NSBA See *National School Boards Association*.

nuclear family A family consisting of two parents and their children.

numerical scale A type of rating scale that uses a fixed number of points to evaluate an individual's ability relative to some performance standard (e.g., 1 = poor, 7 = outstanding). See *checklist* and *descriptive scale*.

nursery school Separately organized and administered school for children of preschool age (i.e., pre-Kindergarteners). Such schools are generally private institutions employing specially trained teachers.

O

object Or object of expenditure, the commodity or service obtained from a specific expenditure; the thing purchased. Objects are classified into categories such as salaries, capital outlay, employee benefits, and materials and supplies. An object of expenditure is commonly referred to as a "line item." See *budget, line-item*.

objective Desired accomplishment or end that is stated explicitly and is capable of being measured. See *goal*.

obligations Organizational commitments, liabilities, or encumbrances that require payment at some future time.

observation techniques Structured methods employed by school supervisors/administrators to observe classroom activities or selected parts of the total school operation.

occupational education Non-academic program of instruction that meets an individual's employment needs by teaching a specific job skill.

O.D. See *organization development*.

"offer versus serve" Federal provision relating to school lunch programs; specifies that middle/senior high school students are not required to accept offered food which they do not plan to eat.

oligarchy Authoritarian leadership by a small group, usually the nobility. In the context of groups, the process of bureaucratization that results when the more indifferent members permit a small, frequently self-sustaining clique to "take charge."

ombudsman An individual authorized to hear and investigate complaints registered by members of an organization about their superiors or the organization per se. Ombudsmen lack line authority; instead, they report findings and make recommendations to a high organizational official. Some ombudsmen are appointed by governments to hear citizen complaints. The ombudsman position originated in Sweden.

open climate One of six *organizational climates* identified through use of the OCDQ. Open climate schools scored as follows on OCDQ subtests: (1) high "esprit"; (2) low "disengagement"; (3) low "hindrance"; (4) average "intimacy"; (5) average "aloofness"; (6) high "consideration"; (7) average "thrust"; and (8) low "production emphasis." See *Organizational Climate Description Questionnaire*.

open door policy Practice, established by management, that provides employees ready access to a superordinate for the purpose of making suggestions, registering complaints, or discussing problems.

open enrollment A procedure that permits students in segregated or overcrowded schools to transfer to other schools within the system.

open meeting laws See *sunshine laws*.

open-records acts Legislation relating to the accessibility and possible release of public records that fall within the public information domain (e.g., names of public employees and their salaries). Such right-to-know laws normally exempt records whose release would constitute violation of privacy.

open shop An organization that neither recognizes nor deals with a labor union. In such situations, union membership is not a condition of employment. See *closed shop* and *union shop*.

open space Or open space plan, architectural term for schools with few or no floor-to-ceiling partitions. In lieu of partitions, screens, cabinets, or other equipment items are used to identify specific instructional areas.

open systems Systems, including human organization systems, that interact with their respective environments (i.e., they have *inputs* and *outputs*). See *inputs-outputs*.

Openness Index A measure of school climate openness or closedness based on selected OCDQ scores. The formula: Openness Index = Thrust

Score + Esprit Score − Disengagement Score. High scores denote an open climate, low scores a closed one. See *Organizational Climate Description Questionnaire*.

operand See *address*.

operating budget A budget which includes all expenditures with the exception of capital outlays; a plan of current expenditures and revenues.

operation code Command (part of an instruction) indicating the operation to be performed by a computer (e.g., "add," "subtract").

Operation Head Start See *Head Start*.

operation of plant An account classification that covers all costs relating to the "housekeeping" of a school system. Included are expenses such as lighting, heating, cleaning supplies, and sanitation.

operational gaming See *game theory*.

operational planning Short-term planning, usually of the day-to-day variety.

operational unit Subdivision of a school system, such as a school, cafeteria program, or athletic department, that: (1) was created to carry out some predetermined major objective, and (2) is separately budgeted.

operations research (OR) A procedure intended to provide management with a viable basis for making plans or arriving at decisions. Mathematical methods and models (e.g., simulation) are employed, these often requiring utilization of the computer.

optimization Strategy/scheme designed to maximize realization of objectives by arranging organizational activities in such a way that they result in an *efficient* operation. Mathematical models are frequently used.

optimum decision The decision reached by choosing the most favorable option from a group of possible options; the decision expected to produce the best possible outcome(s).

optional bonds See *callable bonds*.

optional four-quarter plan See *four-quarter plan*.

order of business Officially adopted sequence in which agenda items are presented and addressed. A sample order of business for a board of education meeting follows: (1) roll call; (2) approval of minutes; (3) report of the superintendent; (4) report of the business manager; (5) letters and communications; (6) unfinished business; (7) new business; and (8) adjournment.

ordinary life See *whole life insurance*.

organic system A term used to describe an organization as a gestalt, an entity made up of several interdependent and interacting subsystems.

organismic study of leadership A study approach based on the notion that several personal variables (e.g., attitudes, values, needs), and not any one personal trait, influence leader behavior; an approach at variance with trait theory. See *trait theory of leadership*.

organization See *formal organization*.

organization chart A graphic depicting the authority relationships between and among members of a formal organization; a portrayal of allocated responsibility. Major duties assigned to each position are sometimes shown.

organization development specialist See *change agent*.

organization, formal See *formal organization*.

organization, horizontal See *horizontal organization*.

organization, informal See *informal organization*.

organization, vertical See *vertical organization*.

organizational behavior Human behavior exhibited by individuals or groups working in formal organizations; behavior resulting from the interaction of an employee and his/her organizational environment.

organizational change Modification of the structure of a formal organization, its goals, or its processes, or of some unit within the organization; sometimes referred to as an organizational innovation. See *innovation*.

organizational climate The total affective system of a group or an organization; the nature and extent to which the internal environment of an organization impacts upon and is perceived by group members and its consequences upon organizational behavior. Contributing to climate are factors such as type of supervision, communication, and the rewards system.

Organizational Climate Description Questionnaire (OCDQ) An instrument, developed by Andrew W. Halpin and Don B. Croft that, based on perceptions of teachers, measures eight aspects of a school's organizational climate. Four relate to *teachers* as a group: "intimacy," "disengagement," "esprit," and "hindrance;" four others focus on the *principal*: "thrust," "consideration," "aloofness," and "production emphasis." See separate definitions of these terms.

organizational conflict See *conflict*.

organizational development (OD) Planned effort to produce change and to improve organizational effectiveness using behavioral science techniques such as behavior modification, interpersonal relations strategies, and team building.

organizational entry Management concept dealing with the manner in which newcomers move into an organization from the outside.

organizational equilibrium See *dynamic equilibrium*.

organizational hierarchy See *hierarchy*.

orientation Personnel program designed to acquaint new employees with the various functions of the employing organization, to inform them of their specific job responsibilities, and to explain the organization's benefits program. Sometimes referred to as *employee induction*.

original entry A student who enters any American public or nonpublic school, elementary or secondary, for the first time.

orthopedically impaired Category of special education students with neuromuscular impairments so severe that they limit the student's educational performance. Included are impairments caused by disease, cerebral palsy, amputation, damage to the central nervous system, and burns.

output The result of an activity. This may take any of several forms such as a tangible product, a service, or a quantity of work. The term may be applied to human accomplishment, a mechanized end product, or data processed by a computer. See *inputs-outputs*.

overhead costs See *indirect costs*.

P

paradigm An idea, theory, or experiment that is presented using a model or graphic.

paraprofessional A full- or part-time staff member who assists a regular teacher but has not earned full professional status. A generic term that, used broadly, may include paid teacher aides, student teachers, and parent volunteers.

parens patriae The right of state governments to take care of persons under their jurisdiction who are unable to direct their own affairs (e.g., the incapacitated, certain minors).

parenting Programs that help parents to become better parents. Such programs include a variety of topics, these frequently reflecting parents' expressed needs (e.g., discipline, communicating with your child, child growth and development).

Parkinson's Law Perhaps the best known of "laws" coined by C. Northcote Parkinson which reads: "Work expands so as to fill the time available for its completion."

parochiaid Government financial assistance to nonpublic schools.

parochial school An educational institution that is church-controlled.

participation leadership A style of leadership in which the leader actively seeks to involve people in decisions whose consequences will affect them.

participatory budget A budget process that involves professional staff, at all levels, as well as representatives of the general public.

paternal climate One of six *organizational climates* identified through use of the OCDQ. Paternal climate schools scored as follows on OCDQ subtests: (1) high "production emphasis"; (2) high "disengagement"; (3) low "hindrance"; (4) low "intimacy"; (5) low "esprit"; (6) average "thrust"; (7) low "aloofness"; and (8) high "consideration." See *Organizational Climate Description Questionnaire.*

path-goal leadership theory A leadership theory, developed by Robert J. House, which suggests that the principal functions of a leader are: (1) to structure and to indicate the "path" by which group members can achieve goals; (2) to facilitate pursuit of the path through clarification and roadblock reduction; and (3) to increase personal rewards once the goals have been attained.

payroll Official listing of wages/salaries earned by employees during a particular time period. Included are deductions for costs such as income tax withholding, Social Security, and insurance.

PDK See *Phi Delta Kappa.*

peer supervision An approach to instructional improvement that involves the free exchange of ideas, methods, and materials among teachers. The "buddy system," in which a novice teacher is assigned to an experienced teacher for resource help, is one manifestation of peer supervision.

per diem Daily rate paid to temporary employees; also, a flat daily rate allowed for employees' and trustees' authorized travel expenses (e.g., meals, lodging).

percolation test A soil test, completed before the start of building construction, that measures the capacity of the soil to absorb water. Such tests yield important information relating to water drainage and/or sewage disposal.

performance In administration, the manner in which, and extent to which the tasks making up one's job are accomplished.

performance audit In education, the observation and assessment of a teacher at work in the classroom, carried out by an appropriate instructional supervisor.

performance bond Certified check or commercial bond, submitted by a contractor working on a school construction project. By presenting such surety, the contractor guarantees that his/her work will be completed in compliance with architectural drawings and specifications.

performance contracting In education, an agreement between a school system and a commercial firm or group of teachers. The firm or teacher group agrees to improve the academic performance of selected students, in specified subjects and in a given period of time, with the understanding that reimbursement will be commensurate with actual achievement as measured on standardized tests.

performance objective The formal statement of a goal and some specified type of performance that will indicate whether or not the desired goal has been reached. Unlike behavioral objectives, which are learner-related, performance objectives are broader in scope and include both learner-related and noninstructional objectives. See *behavioral objective*.

performance standard Indication to an employee of the minimum level of job performance necessary to earn a satisfactory rating. It may be written or oral and may also include specifics such as quality and/ or quantity of work, rate of output, particular tasks to be completed, or time period.

periodical A publication, usually in magazine form, that appears at regular intervals (e.g., monthly, quarterly). Professional journals are classified as periodicals.

permanent certificate In education, a state credential issued to teachers who have fulfilled all requirements for professional recognition. These requirements vary from state to state and frequently call for formal preparation above the baccalaureate level and/or successful teaching experience covering a prescribed period of time.

permanent injunction See *injunction*.

permissive leadership A type of leadership characterized by: (1) little exertion on the part of the leader, and (2) considerable freedom granted to his/her subordinates. Using the "autocratic"-"laissez-faire"-"democratic" leadership typology, permissive leaders fall within the "laissez-faire" category. See *laissez-faire leadership*.

permissive legislation In education, laws that grant decision-making discretion and authority to school districts.

perquisites Special benefits; payments or other benefits/privileges available to top level administrators in addition to regular salary. Example: district vehicle made available for the exclusive use of the superintendent of schools. See *fringe benefits*.

personal leave Leave permitted staff members for personal reasons, including emergencies. Such leaves, if authorized, may: (1) be with or without pay and (2) be limited to a fixed number of days each year.

personal-situational theories Leadership theories which suggest that situations (conditions) prevailing in the organization, in combination with individual (personal) characteristics, may permit an individual to rise to a position of leadership.

personnel administration That part of management having to do with the work of employees and their official relationships with each other. Major functions include: (1) recruitment/selection of employees; (2) training, to improve performance; (3) salary schedule, including fringe benefits; (4) employee evaluation; and (5) personnel record keeping.

personnel evaluation system Or employee evaluation system, a systematic and official appraisal process established to ascertain employee effectiveness. Included among its many characteristics are: its ongoing nature, its dependence on process and product information, its relationship to other administrative processes, and its use of predetermined objectives. The right of rebuttal is frequently extended to those being evaluated.

PERT Acronym for *P*rogram *E*valuation and *R*eview *T*echnique, a management technique for organizing, scheduling, and evaluating the progress of a complex project. Projects are broken down into specific task operations and frequently depicted graphically (i.e., flow-charted).

Peter Principle An organizational principle, authored by Lawrence J. Peter, which reads: "In a hierarchy, each employee tends to rise to his own level of incompetence."

petty cash A small fund of money kept on hand for small and incidental payments.

Phi Delta Kappa (PDK) International professional society for male and female educators. An invitational society; members consist of recognized leaders in education and graduate students who exhibit leadership potential. PDK publishes *Phi Delta Kappan,* newsletters, books, monographs, and fastbacks.

picketing A type of employee demonstration that involves patrolling near an employer's premises for any or all of several reasons: (1) calling a labor dispute to the attention of the public; (2) discouraging patrons from entering the premises; (3) encouraging employees to join/form a labor organization; or (4) persuading an employer to take some desired action.

Pilot A specialized and relatively simple computer language used to develop CAI (computer-assisted instruction) courseware.

pilot program A new, experimental, and usually small program introduced to demonstrate and/or test new procedures/approaches.

pin map See *spot map.*

"place-bound" administrators A term coined by Richard O. Carlson to describe school administrators who generally remain in one school system, waiting for the superintendency to become vacant. Unlike "career-bound" administrators, they do not move to other systems to achieve advancement. If appointed to the top position, "place-bound" administrators usually do not move on to other superintendencies. See *"career-bound" administrators.*

placement (1) A personnel service that helps candidates find jobs. (2) In the context of contingency theory, placement refers to the matching of a leader possessing a particular leadership style with a job situation that calls for such a style. (3) The assignment of students to particular classes or grade levels.

planning An element of the administrative process concerned with the identification and realization of goals. Specific steps are: (1) goal identification; (2) assessment of present situation; (3) determining the most effective steps/strategies for realizing goals; (4) implementation of these steps/strategies; and, (5) evaluation.

planning, programming, budgeting system (PPBS) Also known as Planning, Programming, Budgeting, Evaluation System (PPBES), an integrated budget system in which allocations are determined on the basis of specific program objectives. Program performance is subsequently analyzed, and future year implications determined, by examining the extent to which such goals have been achieved.

plant See *school plant*.

PLATO Acronym for *P*rogrammed *L*ogic for *A*utomated *T*eaching *O*perations, a computer-assisted instructional system developed in 1960 and usable with pupils of most ages.

platoon school See *Gary Plan*.

Plowden Report Report on British primary school programs and practices (1967), prepared by the British Central Advisory Council for Education; named for its chairperson, Lady Plowden.

point of entry In the context of change, the organizational level to which a change agent first directs his/her attention and efforts.

policy Official guideline for carrying out action. Policies constitute the aims/intentions of an organization. They are usually formulated by a governing body for the purpose of guiding administrative decision-making. In school systems, policies are adopted by boards of education and are subsequently implemented by the school administrators.

portable building Structure capable of being moved from one site to another without disassembly. In education, "portable classrooms" are among the most frequently used portable buildings.

Portland Plan A plan for organizing curriculum in a nine-year elementary school, introduced into the Portland, Oregon schools in 1897. Total curriculum was divided into 54 units, with 6 units to be completed per year by most students. Brighter pupils were permitted to complete all units in seven years.

POSDCORB An acronym formulated in the 1930's by Lyndall Urwick to describe the work of the chief executive. The first letters of seven types of administrative activity are combined to form the acronym. The activities: *p*lanning, *o*rganizing, *s*taffing, *d*irecting, *co*-ordinating, *r*eporting, and *b*udgeting.

position One's rank/title in a hierarchy; sometimes used as a synonym for "office." In organizations, specific roles are associated with each position, these indicating both behavior expectations as well as the position-holder's role relationship to others. See *role*.

position description See *job description*.

position specification See *job specification*.

post-audit Review of an organization's financial records after a project (including all related transactions) has been completed. Its principal purposes are to: (1) check on decisions made; (2) ensure that all expenditures were authorized and legal; and (3) ensure that internal accounting controls are being used properly.

post-observation conference Individual conference with a teacher immediately following a formal classroom observation. Included among its purposes are: (1) to review and analyze the observation, noting strengths and weaknesses; (2) to identify approaches/strategies for correcting weaknesses; and (3) to encourage innovative teaching. See *clinical supervision* and *pre-observation conference*.

posting In accounting, the process of transferring detailed information from a journal, cash register, or similar document to the ledger.

postsecondary education Instruction received at a public or private institution of higher education (e.g., college, technical school, university) by a person who has completed a high school program.

power The potential to induce or influence another. In organizations, the capability, inherent or acquired, to direct others toward realization of goals or objectives. See *coercive power, expert power, legitimate power, referent power,* and *reward power*.

power, discretionary See *discretionary duty*.

power structures Influential individuals, interest groups, and organizational/community members who, formally or informally, have the potential for influencing the outcomes of major decisions.

powers, ministerial See *ministerial duty*.

PPBS See *planning-programming-budgeting system*.

pre-audit Review of a proposed expenditure by a comptroller or other designated official; an examination of financial transactions before they are completed.

preferential hiring (1) More favorable hiring treatment granted to minority job applicants because of their sex, race, religion, national origin, or color; an illegal practice except when employment quotas have been mandated by the courts. (Not to be confused with special minority recruitment efforts.) (2) In collective bargaining, agreement by an employer to give preference to members of an employee organization when filling job vacancies.

preliminary drawings See *schematic drawings*.

premium Amount paid for insurance by a policyholder; can usually be paid annually, semi-annually, quarterly, or monthly.

pre-observation conference Individual conference with a teacher prior to a formal classroom observation. Its purpose is to: (1) establish rapport with the teacher; (2) identify activities to be observed; and (3) review the procedures to be used for recording and assessing such activities. See *clinical supervision* and *post-observation conference*.

preprimary school A separately organized school for students who have yet to enroll in the first grade (i.e., Kindergarteners and pre-Kindergarteners).

preschool education Or preschool program, organized learning experiences for children who have yet to enroll in grade 1. (Some definitions delimit the age range to birth-to-age 5.) Instruction is carried out in groups, under the tutelage of a qualified teacher. Examples of preschool education include nursery schools and the Head Start program.

primary group A group whose members enjoy a close-knit, warm, and emotionally satisfying relationship. Examples include families, friendship groups, and cliques. See *secondary group*.

primary level The lower grades of an elementary school, K–3 or 1–3.

primary school A separately administered school that enrolls only primary level students (i.e., students in grades K–3 or 1–3).

Princeton Plan The pairing of two physically proximate schools, one with a predominantly white enrollment, the other with mostly black students, for the purpose of achieving racial desegregation; named for Princeton, New Jersey, where the plan was initiated. Usually, primary grade children from both schools are assigned to one building, all intermediate level students to the other.

principal Administrative head of a school who, subject to school system policy, manages the school's total program. Principals normally report to the superintendent of schools or to some other central office administrator designated by the superintendent.

principal investigator See *project director*.

principle General law or truth; a general statement describing some particular mode of behavior, process, or property relating to natural phenomena.

printout The output of a computer that has been printed on paper.

prior service Years of employment accumulated prior to present employment. Depending on law and local policies, such service may be credited toward current salary, seniority, or retirement.

private school A nonpublic educational institution supported by other than public monies. Such institutions are operated by individuals or nonpublic agencies/organizations. This generic term includes parochial, independent, and proprietary schools operating at all instructional levels. See *independent school, parochial school,* and *proprietary school*.

probationary status Employment status of an employee who is employed on a year-to-year basis during which time his/her eligibility for permanent status is being determined.

probationary teacher A teacher not yet tenured or eligible for continuing contract but who is working to obtain tenure by serving a probationary period.

procedural due process A proceeding (hearing) in which an individual, after having been given appropriate notice, is given the opportunity to defend him/herself and otherwise to protect his/her rights before a tribunal; includes the right to be aided by counsel. See *substantive due process*.

procedure A predetermined, systematic method for accomplishing a stated objective, and doing so in as efficient a manner as possible.

process The ways and means by which objectives are attained; a systematic series of steps/actions leading one to a desired outcome or end-product.

process evaluation Appraisal made on the basis of means (i.e., procedures) rather than ends. For example, process evaluation takes place when a principal makes judgements about a teacher based on teaching methods used. Often contrasted with "product evaluation." See *product evaluation*.

product That which results from process; an outcome.

product evaluation Appraisal made on the basis of some output or product data, often tangible. In education, evaluations of teachers based on student learning (i.e., achievement) illustrate product evaluation. Often contrasted with "process evaluation." See *process evaluation*.

production emphasis One of four "principal behavior" dimensions (subtests) included in the OCDQ. The term is used to describe the school principal whose administrative style is highly directive. Teachers are closely supervised; one-way communication (i.e., principal-to-teacher) prevails, with little regard for feedback. See *Organizational Climate Description Questionnaire*.

profession An occupation that requires advanced education and specialized training. Professionals (e.g., doctors, lawyers) tend to: (1) possess a unique body of knowledge; (2) have a code of ethical behavior; (3) be self-policing and (4) be self-governing.

professional leave See *sabbatical leave*.

professional negotiation A procedure through which teacher associations and school boards discuss and eventually agree upon matters of concern to both (e.g., salary scales, grievance procedures). The term "professional negotiation" was first used in education by the National Education Association as a substitute for the traditional union term, "collective bargaining."

professional sanctions Strategy advocated by the National Education Association that involves censure and wide dissemination of information regarding purportedly unfair labor practices by a school, school district, or community. Withholding of services is recommended; prospective employees are urged not to seek employment in such agencies/locations.

program (1) In teaching, an instructional plan (e.g., syllabus) covering a prescribed body of material to be taught. (2) In management, a sequence of activities or decision-making steps leading toward completion of a desired goal. (3) In data processing, a series of instructions to be carried out by a computer. (4) In budgeting, a carefully defined cost center based on organizational units, functions, or activities.

program budget See *budget, program*.

Program Evaluation and Review Technique See *PERT*.

programmed instruction A training process that presents subject matter using automated methods (i.e., teaching machines, programmed texts). Material to be learned is presented in sequential steps. Instant feedback tells the student whether or not a question has been answered correctly.

programmed learning Detailed and usually sequential learning exercises that use a series of branched responses and/or statements that permit the student, on a self-paced basis, to progress through the study material.

progressive tax A graduated tax that exacts a higher percentage (rate) of high incomes than of low incomes. An example is the federal income tax under which high-income taxpayers pay a larger percentage of their incomes than do low-income taxpayers. See *regressive tax*.

project director The individual responsible for managing a project. In the context of grantsmanship, the project director (sometimes referred to as the "principal investigator") plans and prepares grant proposals. If and when the proposal is funded, he/she is responsible for carrying it out.

promotion Advancement in status or position; opposite of demotion. Examples: (1) advancement of a pupil to the next higher grade level, or (2) advancement of a principal to the post of assistant superintendent.

property accounting In education, a record keeping process undertaken to provide accurate information for planning, managing, and evaluating school property (i.e., buildings, sites, and equipment).

property tax A tax levied at a uniform rate on property (usually real property) by a board of education or other fiscally independent governmental unit. This tax is the primary source of funds, raised locally, to finance public schools.

Proposition 2½ A referendum, approved by Massachusetts' voters (November 1980) that placed limits on various tax rates. The best known of the proposition's several limits was the one that placed a lid on the property tax levy, limiting it to 2½% of the property's market value.

Proposition 13 Or the Jarvis-Gann Property-Tax Initiative, California legislation (1978) that places a limitation on the revenue-generating ability of the state and local governments, including school districts; a measure designed to reduce existing property taxes and to limit future property tax increases. See *tax limitations*.

proprietary account See *account*.

proprietary school A school operated for profit. Such institutions often seek out markets not served by neighboring public schools.

proscenium Architect's term for that part of a stage situated in front of the curtain.

protected classes Members of a minority group who, in past years, experienced job discrimination but are now protected against such practices by Title VII of the 1964 Civil Rights Act (amended).

protest school Synonym for "nonpublic school." The term, used less frequently today than it was even 30 years ago, refers to the enrollment option parents enjoy namely, to "protest" the public school by sending their children to a nonpublic school at their own expense.

protocol materials Filmed or videotaped segments depicting teacher behavior, recorded as the teacher interacts with students. Such materials are used in teacher training programs to relate practice with concepts studied on campus.

provisional certificate Temporary credential issued to an educational practitioner who has yet to meet all requirements for permanent licensure.

proximate cause Key issue in many negligence actions; an element of tort liability. Defined in *Ballentine's Law Dictionary* (p. 1017) as "that cause, which, in natural and continuous sequence, unbroken by any efficient intervening cause, produces the injury, and without which the result would not have occurred." See *negligence*.

psychomotor domain One of three behavior domains making up a taxonomy developed by Benjamin Bloom, et al. (1956). Behaviors within this domain are concerned primarily with psychological effects upon physical activity (i.e., motor skills and motor coordination). See *affective domain* and *cognitive domain*.

Public Law 94-142 Or the Education for all Handicapped Children Act (1975), federal legislation assuring free appropriate public education to all handicapped children; covers all exceptionalities except for the gifted.

public relations Information which an organization disseminates to its public(s). A conscious and frequently sustained effort on the part of an organization to: (1) acquaint others with its performance and achievements, and (2) influence their perception of and attitudes toward the organization. See *school community relations*.

public school An educational institution that is supported primarily by public funds and operated by legally elected or appointed representatives of the citizenry.

Pueblo Plan Approach to organizing elementary and secondary schools, introduced into the Pueblo, Colorado schools (1888) by Superintendent Preston W. Search. Although grade levels were retained, the program of instruction was individualized; pupils progressed at their own rate.

punched card A card in which holes are punched for the purpose of recording data. Each hole is coded to represent a specific piece of information. Such cards can be processed: (1) manually, using a needle; (2) visually; or (3) mechanically (e.g., using a computer reader).

punishment-centered rules According to Alvin Gouldner, a category of rules whose violation results in punishment and precipitates tension when enforced. An illustration of such rules: required punching of a time-clock each morning. See *mock rules* and *representative rules*.

punitive damages See *damages*.

pupil accounting See *student accounting*.

pupil activity fund See *student activity fund*.

pupil capacity See *normal capacity*.

pupil personnel services See *student personnel services*.

pupil-teacher ratio Or student-teacher ratio, the total number of students in a school or school system divided by the total number of teachers, expressed in full-time equivalency terms, who are assigned to the same school or school system.

pupil transportation services General term for activities relating to the transporting of students to and from school. Included are: (1) legally required home-school-home trips; (2) school-sponsored field trips; and (3) travel related to interscholastic athletics.

pupil unit of measure Standard educational measure based on a pupil factor. Pupil unit measures may be reported as of a given point in time (e.g., total attendance, total membership) or for a specified period (e.g., average daily attendance, average daily membership).

pupil weighting See *weighted pupil measures*.

purchase order Written request to a vendor for specified materials or services to be delivered at a set price.

Q

qualified privilege A doctrine of law that permits public officials, including school board members, to exchange information in open discussion without fear of libel. Such immunity applies so long as the information is necessary, relevant, and not intended to malign others.

quality control A monitoring procedure designed to insure that predetermined standards are being maintained.

quartiles The three points that divide numbers, scores, or cases in a distribution into four equal parts. The first quartile (Ql) is equivalent to the 25th percentile, the second (Q2) to the median, and the third (Q3) to the 75th percentile.

queuing theory A mathematical analysis, developed in 1917 by A. K. Erland of Denmark, that is used to reduce the costs of waiting in line. In education, it may be used to study and reduce cafeteria, registration, basketball ticket, and other such lines.

quick ratio See *current ratio*.

Quincy Grammar School First graded school (i.e., one teacher per grade level), established (1848) in Boston by John D. Philbrick.

quinmester plan A calendar arrangement that divides the school year into five nine-week sessions, Each session consists of 45 school days. Students meet state attendance requirements by enrolling in any four sessions of their own choosing.

quo warranto Litigation that challenges an elected or appointed official's legal right to hold office. Also included are challenges that question the legality of an agency such as a school district. Bases for such challenges may include purported lack of qualifications or election/appointment/creation irregularities.

quorum The number of members required to be present for business to be transacted legally by a board or other organization. Under the common law, a quorum is a simple majority. Unless specified otherwise by law, action by a school board is legal if supported by a majority vote.

R

racial balance A goal of school desegregation. Two widely-used definitions are: (1) the assignment of students such that no more than 50% of a school's enrollment is made up of minority students, and (2) the distribution of students such that the racial/ethnic makeup of each school is fairly representative of the racial/ethnic makeup of the total community. See *integration, racial.*

racial integration See *integration, racial.*

random access See *dial access.*

rank and file Labor relations term applied to the membership of a labor organization, exclusive of its leaders and employers.

rank-in-class (R:C) Academic standing of a student relative to his/her classmates, expressed as a rank-order and normally based on cumulative grade point average. One of several predictive measures used by college admissions officials to project an applicant's likelihood of success in college.

ratification In labor relations, the formal endorsement (frequently via ballot) of a negotiated agreement by eligible members of a labor organization.

rating scale Instrument used for the systematic recording of opinions concerning the characteristics/behaviors of an individual. See *checklist, descriptive scale,* and *numerical scale.*

ratio I.Q. See *intelligence quotient.*

ratio salary schedule See *indexed salary schedule*.

real property Land and physical improvements on the land.

recall election An election conducted for the purpose of removing public office-holders during their terms of office. Several states prescribe procedures that need to be followed to remove elected officials (including school board members) from office. The first such procedure is commonly a petition signed by a fixed percentage of the electorate.

receipts Accounting term for cash received.

reciprocity In education, an interstate agreement, to which many states are parties, that facilitates the movement of certified teachers from one state to another. Certificates are most likely to be issued to out-of-state teachers trained in institutions accredited by the National Council for the Accreditation of Teacher Education.

recognition In labor relations, official acknowledgement by an employer that an employee organization has the right to negotiate for its members (sometimes, for all employees).

recruitment The process of locating prospective, qualified employees; a personnel administration function.

reduction in force (RIF) Planned decrease in the number of employees usually resulting from enrollment decreases and/or economic factors. Policies and procedures, when established, contain guidelines/criteria for the administrator faced with the task of discharging employees and/or reducing the number of positions.

referendum The process of having the electorate vote on substantive issues (e.g., increasing the ceiling on school tax rates) previously proposed or approved by an authorized governmental agency. See *initiative*.

referent power The power an organizational member enjoys because others either like or identify with him/her. One of five power classifications formulated by John R. P. French, Jr. and Bertram Raven. See *coercive power, expert power, legitimate power,* and *reward power*.

referral Recommendation of an individual to a physician, health agency, etc. for the purpose of evaluation and/or treatment. School counselors, speech therapists, psychologists, nurses and other specialists routinely initiate and receive referrals of pupils.

refunding bonds Bonds with later maturities that are used to replace (i.e., pay off) existing bonds. The refunding action may be taken for any of several reasons (e.g., to save interest charges, to extend the period of existing debt).

regional district A separate high school district formed when two or more school districts consolidate their secondary school programs. Under such arrangements, the original districts continue to operate their own elementary schools. An organizational structure found in a limited number of states.

register In accounting, the book in which certain financial transactions, documents, and events are recorded; may or may not be a journal.

register of attendance Or attendance register, official document used to record basic student enrollment and attendance information. Data recorded usually include: (1) name, address, sex, and birthdate of each student; (2) date student entered or withdrew from school; and (3) dates on which each student was present, absent, or tardy. In recent years, data processing systems have been developed to expedite the collection and recording of such information.

registered bond A bond containing the name of its owner. Interest is paid only to the registered owner. Such bonds contrast with unregistered, or "bearer bonds" which can be transferred readily from one individual to another. See *coupon bond*.

regressive tax A tax whose rate is inversely related to "ability to pay." Such taxes exact a larger share (proportion) of income from low-income taxpayers than from high-income taxpayers. Examples of the regressive tax are the excise tax, sales tax, and property tax. See *progressive tax*.

regular day school A nonresidential elementary or secondary school offering instruction above the Kindergarten level.

regulation An order intended to regulate conduct and usually possessing the force of law. Regulations may derive from sources such as a statute, an ordinance, or action by a governing board. Commonly used as a synonym for "rule." See *rules*.

reimbursable fund See *revolving fund*.

released time Arrangements between public school and church officials which permit public school students to leave school for a specific time period to receive religious instruction. Instruction is provided by church authorities, usually toward the close of the school day. Non-participating students are required to spend the full day in school.

reliability In statistics, the consistency with which a test meaures that which it was intended to measure. The extent of reliability is usually expressed using some form of reliability coefficient or standard error of measurement.

remunerative power See *compliance typology*.

reorder point In supply management, the time when utilization rate and lead time information indicate to a purchasing agent that the time has come to reorder (i.e., replenish) stock.

reorganization of districts See *consolidation*.

replacement cost The actual price one must pay to replace an asset (e.g., school building, equipment) with another that is equal in kind and quality.

reporting period The specific block of time covered in a report (e.g., month, semester, fiscal year).

representative rules Rules that, according to Alvin Gouldner, are obeyed by employees and enforced by management. Because of their inherent worthwhileness, their enforcement generates little or no anxiety. In schools, an illustration of such rules is the "no talking during school fire drills" regulation. See *mock rules* and *punishment-centered rules*.

request for proposal (RFP) Printed announcement by a funding agency detailing: (1) the availability of funds for a particular kind of project; (2) specific delimitations (e.g., time limits, populations to be served); (3) criteria for evaluation of proposals; (4) deadlines for submission of proposals; and (5) other related information.

requisition A written request for specified articles or services. Such requests originate with one school official and are directed to another school official (e.g., purchasing officer) or to another department.

resegregation Segregation (racial, ethnic) of students that takes place as a result of population shifts after the school system has been desegregated.

reserve In financial accounting, an amount set aside for specified use at some future time.

residence A student's domicile. The domicile's physical location (i.e., in-district or out-of-district) is used to determine whether or not the student may attend local public schools on a tuition-free basis.

resident student A student whose legal residence is located within the geographical area served by a school, a school district, or an institution. State colleges and universities normally define a resident student as one who has an in-state domicile and who has resided in that state for at least twelve consecutive months.

residential school A school in which students are boarded (e.g., state school for the deaf).

residential treatment center Or residential treatment facility, a residential institution that provides some form of treatment. Primary attention is given to treatment rather than instruction.

resignation Voluntary and permanent termination of employment by an employee.

resource teacher Specialist who works with students with special learning needs; also provides consultative assistance to the students' regular teachers. He/she may work in the regular classroom or in a "resource room" to which individual or small groups of students come for special help.

respondeat superior Legal doctrine which holds that an employer is liable for the acts of the employee.

résumé Written summary of an individual's personal, educational, and professional qualifications such as his/her job experience. The résumé is frequently prepared by job applicants to supplement information noted on a prospective employer's standard application form.

retention See *nonpromotion*.

retention rate (1) The percentage of all students in an entering class completing a program of studies within the prescribed period of time. (2) The recall of learned materials at different time intervals.

retirement Voluntary or compulsory termination of employment upon reaching a fixed age or because of sickness/disability. Eligibility is determined by policy or law.

retirement fund A type of trust fund, developed through employee and/or employer contributions; used for the purpose of distributing retirement annuities and related benefits to participants who have become eligible for retirement. Retirement systems in which public school teachers participate include: (1) state systems for teachers only; (2) state systems for all state employees; and (3) local (e.g., city) systems.

retraining The preparation of an employee for a new position, one for which he/she was not previously trained.

retrieval See *information retrieval*.

revaluation The assignment of a new value to an asset (e.g., increasing the assessed valuation of a residence).

revenue gap The budgetary discrepancy that exists when projected expenditures exceed anticipated revenues. For school districts, such gaps are prohibited by law, a fact necessitating either of two remedies: (1) increases in revenues, or (2) expenditure reductions.

revenue sharing A plan for distributing a portion of federal revenues to state and local governments unconditionally. Its principal purpose is to decentralize decision-making by letting local governments decide how public monies are to be spent.

revenues Receipts, or income; the opposite of "expenditures." Major revenue sources for school systems are proceeds from property taxes and state aid.

revolving fund Or reimbursable fund, fund that is continually replenished by earnings from operations or transfers from other funds. As a result, the original amount remains intact.

reward power The power one has in an organization that derives from his/her ability to reward others (e.g., dole out favors, salary increases, promotions). One of five forms of power identified by John R. P.

French, Jr. and Bertram Raven. See *coercive power, expert power, legitimate power,* and *referent power.*

RFP See *request for proposal.*

rider Addendum to a contract, usually separate page(s) to be attached to the original contract.

RIFing See *reduction in force.*

right-to-work laws Legislation outlawing collective bargaining agreements that require an individual to join a union or other employees' organization in order to secure or to hold his/her job.

role Behaviors expected of an individual occupying a particular organizational position (e.g., principal, counselor). "Role" should not be confused with "position," a term that refers to one's job title alone. For example, an individual may hold the position of middle school principal, but owing to inexperience, lack of ability, or other inhibiting reasons, may not be able to fulfill the role of principal. See *position.*

role ambiguity A condition resulting from the fact that roles are not defined clearly. The individual either is not told or is not certain what he/she is expected to do.

role conflict Situation that arises when: (1) an individual is obligated to perform two distinct roles that are competing or incompatible; (2) the individual receives incompatible or incongruent definitions/expectations of his/her role from different groups; and, (3) the source of differing role definitions/expectations comes from the same group. See *inter-role conflict* and *intra-role conflict.*

role description The actual (i.e., observed) behavior of an individual who is performing his/her role.

role expectation Normative prerogatives and duties of an officeholder; the anticipated role behavior that a person has of an individual occupying a particular organizational position. A principal, for example, has certain expectations of the superintendent, and vice-versa.

role perception The manner in which a role incumbent (e.g., superintendent, school psychologist) thinks others expect him/her to behave.

role-personality conflict Condition that exists when role expectations and the personality of the role incumbent are not congruent; a serious problem when variations between these two dimensions are extreme.

role retention The assertion and practice of leadership rather than ceding leadership to others.

role theory A theoretical approach that examines the behavior of individuals who occupy various positions in a formal organization. The organization is viewed as a miniature society within which these individuals operate.

rotation The practice of transferring employees to new positions/locations/organizational units. Rationale for this practice includes the need: (1) to overcome boredom; (2) to permit the employee to become acquainted with other jobs/units within the organization; and (3) skill improvement.

rules Directives indicating the kind of behavior that should or should not be expected, on certain kinds of occasion, of a particular person or persons in general. A standard of correctness; not a command. Sometimes used as a synonym for statements prescribing the manner in which policies and plans are to be implemented. See *mock rules, representative rules* and *punishment-centered rules*; also see *regulation*.

runoff election In collective bargaining, a second election conducted when the first produces no union with a majority in a representation election. When more than two unions are competing for such recognition, the runoff may be restricted to the two receiving the highest number of votes in the initial election.

S

sabbatical leave Leave normally granted to professional employees who have completed six or more years of full-time service. Such leaves are intended to increase employees' value to their organization, their clients, and themselves through professional renewal activities such as study, travel, research, and writing.

salary differential In education, the term used to describe differences in salary accounted for by differences in levels of training. As used in the single salary schedule, an "increment" is granted for each year of experience, a "differential" for variations in training (e.g., B.A. vs. M.A. vs. Ph.D.). See *salary increment*.

salary increment Regular increase in pay that has been incorporated into a salary schedule; commonly found in salary schedules of school districts and other governmental agencies. In the single salary schedule for teachers, "increments" are paid for each year of experience, "differentials" for different levels of training. See *salary differential*.

sales tax Tax levied by many states and some local governments upon the sale of goods at the retail level; a regressive tax. See *regressive tax*.

sanctions Penalties or censure used to enforce conformity to group (e.g., organizational) norms. See *professional sanctions*.

Santa Barbara Plan Elementary school organization plan, introduced into the Santa Barbara schools (1898) by Fred Burke. Curriculum was divided into three courses—for slow, average, and bright pupils. The plan featured promotion three times each year; nonpromotion was eliminated.

satisfaction In leadership theory, the extent to which the role requirements of a leader accord with his/her personal need-dispositions.

satisficing decisions Decisions deemed to be satisfactory. Although they may not lead to optimal outcomes, they do fulfill a minimum standard. Such decisions may be revised in the future should such action be deemed necessary.

satisfiers One of two motivation categories ("satisfiers" and "dissatisfiers"), identified by Frederick Herzberg, that bear on job performance. Factors included in his "satisfier" classification are: achievement, recognition, work itself, responsibility, advancement, and growth. See *dissatisfiers*.

saturation study A community analysis that projects maximum land use in a school district; from this, future population size is inferred. A basis for determining future school building needs.

save harmless laws Statutes, passed in some states, that protect school district employees found to be negligent in the discharge of their duties. Where such laws have been passed, districts are either authorized or required to assume full liability (i.e., to pay any judgments) for the actions of their employees.

scab An employee who works during a strike or fills in for a striking employee.

scalar principle A concept of management, proposed by Henri Fayol, in which: (1) positions are arranged hierarchically, in chain-of-command fashion, to indicate superior-subordinate relationships; (2) emphasis is on authority; and (3) responsibilities are well defined for each position.

scale A carefully sequenced group of numbers whose values indicate the extent of factors such as intelligence, a trait, a characteristic, or a phenomenon. Examples: (1) thermometer, used to measure temperature, and (2) I.Q. score, used to measure intelligence.

SCDE's Acronym for *s*chools, *c*olleges, and *d*epartments of *e*ducation in institutions of higher education.

schedule, conventional See *conventional schedule*.

schedule, modular See *modular schedule*.

schedule of progress A chart, normally prepared by the school architect, that shows: (1) planned time allotted for each phase of school construction, and (2) actual time recorded for each phase. Such charts make it possible to tell whether or not a construction project is on schedule.

schedule, variable See *variable schedule*.

schematic drawings Preliminary, "rough" drawings prepared by an architect during the design stage of a school or other building.

school An educational institution, organized as a single unit and usually housed in one building. Its teachers offer specific kinds of instruction to a particular student population. In some cases, two schools (e.g., elementary and middle) may be housed in the same building. The term is sometimes used to designate an institution, other times a building.

school attendance area See *attendance area*.

school attendance unit See *attendance unit*.

school-based management Procedure for decentralizing school system decision-making. As much authority as possible is assigned to individual principals for management of their respective schools. They, in turn, are expected to involve teachers and local citizens in decisions affecting budgets, personnel, and curricula.

school board See *board of education, local*.

school business administration Management of the business operations of a school system. This responsibility, frequently assigned to a school business administrator, may be shared with the superintendent and/or the school board's fiscal officer. Major tasks performed by the school business administrator include: financial accounting, purchasing and stores, food services, buildings and grounds administration, data processing, grantsmanship, and office management.

school census Periodic (usually annual) or continuous canvass, carried out on a house-to-house basis, for the purpose of ascertaining facts such as the names, addresses, ages, and grade levels of children and youth residing within a geographic area served by a school or school system.

school code School laws of a state usually collated and published in book form.

school community relations The interaction between a school and its public (including parents and nonparents); a program in which community residents are actively engaged in the affairs of the school. Unlike public relations, which is limited to communications from school to community, school community relations implies a partnership between the two. See *public relations*.

school district Or school system, a governmental unit, governed by a board of education, and charged by the state with responsibility for controlling public elementary and/or secondary education at the local level; also known as the "local basic administrative unit." In 1983, there were approximately 16,000 school districts in the United States.

school district reorganization See *consolidation*.

school management The process of leading people to achieve effective school operation. Key elements are planning and control; emphasis is frequently placed on people rather than things.

school personnel Generic term that includes three categories of school employees: (1) teachers; (2) those who render instructional support services to teachers; and (3) administrators.

school plant School building; more specifically, the building, the site on which it has been erected, and all facilities used in supporting the school program.

school plant planning Planning for educational facilities. The procedure is normally a complex one involving steps such as surveys, population projections, solicitation of community residents and faculty for advice, architectural consultations, renderings, financing, and scheduling.

school site A piece of land and all improvements to it (structures excepted); land that is, or is likely to be used for school building purposes. Improvements may include parking areas, landscaping, playfields, grading, and drainage.

school tax rate See *tax rate*.

school term See *term*.

school trustee Synonym for school board member. In independent schools, one who has fiduciary or policy responsibility.

school vandalism See *vandalism*.

school-within-a-school Method of overcoming the disadvantages inherent in relatively large schools. The large building is divided into two or more components, or mini-schools, each with its own regular teachers, counselor(s), and administrative coordinator. Mini-schools share common facilities (e.g., gymnasium) and, in some cases, teachers of special subjects (e.g., vocational education).

scientific management A management philosophy, developed by Frederick W. Taylor, that stressed maximum worker efficiency (i.e., task specialization) as the means for realizing organizational objectives. Popular in the late 19th and early 20th century, scientific management emphasized: (1) division of work, including specification/prescription of work and tools; (2) proper matching of workers and jobs; (3) management-worker cooperation; (4) rewards based on performance; and (5) specialized supervision.

scope In curriculum, the range or breadth of content making up a course or instructional unit, sometimes referred to as the "what" of curriculum. Frequently contrasted with "sequence," a term that indicates the ordering (i.e., "when") of material to be taught. See *sequence*.

search and seizure In school law, the act of examining a student's property (e.g., locker, purse) or person for the purpose of uncovering weapons, drugs, stolen property, etc. Since unreasonable searches may violate the U.S. Constitution's Fourth Amendment, recommended guidelines need to be followed to insure that the student's Constitutional rights are protected.

secondary group Group organized to serve a particular purpose (e.g., members of an academic department, custodial crew, committee members). Such groups do not normally enjoy the close-knit, warm, and emotionally satisfying relationship manifest in "primary" groups. See *primary group*.

secondary school A school offering a post-elementary school program; a generic term that includes middle schools, junior high schools, and senior high schools.

secretary of the board See *clerk, school board*.

secured bond Bond that is backed by an asset (e.g., mortgage, collateral). In case of default, bond holders may initiate foreclosure proceedings and liquidate real property for restitution purposes.

segregated school A school whose students and/or teachers have been physically separated from each other on the basis of race or ethnic origin. See *de facto segregation* and *de jure segregation*.

selection In personnel administration, the choosing, from a pool of candidates, the one(s) most likely to succeed.

self-contained classroom Method of organizing students for instruction. One teacher, a generalist, is responsible for teaching all or most subjects to a single group of students, for a major part of the school day, during the entire school year. It is the most commonly used organization plan used in American elementary schools.

self-insurance Insurance program engaged in by some large school systems. Rather than participating in commercial or state insurance programs, self-insuring systems may: (1) carry no insurance, preferring to pay for financial losses out of current funds; (2) carry some insurance to provide high-risk protection; or (3) establish their own insurance reserve out of which financial losses are paid. Policies held in commercial companies are phased out as the self-insurance reserves increase.

self-study See *institutional self-study*.

senior high school Secondary school normally enrolling students in grades 8–12 or 9–12; a receiving school for middle school or junior high school graduates.

seniority Length of service with one employer or organization; sometimes, length of continuous service. Seniority may afford varying degrees of job security to senior employees during layoff periods and, in some instances, gives them added consideration when promotion opportunities occur.

sensitivity training A small-group training method (e.g., T-Groups) designed to help participants understand: (1) their own interpersonal behavior; (2) the behavior of others; or (3) communication techniques. At different times, participants become both experimenters and subjects. See *T-group*.

separate-but-equal doctrine A legal doctrine, ruled unconstitutional in 1954, that holds that equal treatment (i.e., programs substantially similar in quality) is possible even though students are assigned to separate schools on the basis of race.

separation Termination of one's employment for any reason (e.g., retirement, dismissal, resignation).

separation interview See *exit interview*.

serial bonds Bonds whose principal plus accrued interest is repaid in periodic installments over the term of the issue. Installments are normally paid out of revenues of the fiscal year in which they fall due. Serial bonds are numbered and retired in numerical order.

sequence In curriculum, the order in which subject content is arranged and to be presented. See *scope*.

seriously emotionally disturbed Category of special education students who, over time and to a significant degree, exhibit one or more of the following characteristics: (1) inability to learn, unexplainable by intellectual, sensory, or health factors; (2) inability to maintain satisfactory interpersonal relationships; (3) inappropriate behavior under normal circumstances; (4) pervasive mood of unhappiness or depression; or (5) tendency to develop physical symptoms/fears associated with personal or school problems.

settlement Common agreement reached through negotiation.

severance pay Payment made to an employee who either has been discharged for reasons beyond his/her control (e.g., when a contract has been cut short) or has completed his/her employment contract.

sex equity Gender equity; provides that all students/employees should have equal opportunity and enjoy equal services according to their individual abilities/interests, not because they are a male or female.

sex fair The practice of treating both sexes in as equal a manner as possible.

shared facilities Public school buildings, sites, or equipment used, rent-free, by nonpublic school students who are under the direct supervision of nonpublic school officials; or, comparable facilities, owned by a nonpublic school, that public school pupils, supervised by public school personnel, use without rental fee.

shared services Arrangement whereby the services of one school or school system are made available to another school or school system on a no-cost basis. The term usually applies to services (e.g., nursing) that public school personnel provide to a neighboring nonpublic school, at either location.

shared time Or dual enrollment, an arrangement in which a student attends two schools concurrently (with parental permission). A common pattern is that of a parochial school student who attends a public school part-time (e.g., afternoons) for specialized instruction not available in the parochial school. Another arrangement: a public school student who attends an area vocational high school for part of the day. Less frequently, a student enrolled in one public school may attend another public school for specialized instruction.

sheltered workshop An employment facility, usually located in the local community, that provides employment opportunities/protection to handicapped individuals who are unable to compete with nonhandicapped individuals in the open market.

shop steward See *steward*.

sick leave Time away from work that has been granted to an employee because of his/her illness, accident, or related disability. See *sick pay*.

sick pay Salary paid to an employee who is not able to work because of illness or accident.

sickout Work stoppage that occurs when large numbers of employees purport that they are too sick to be able to report for work. In such cases, employers frequently insist on medical verification to justify each employee's absence.

simulation The study of real problems using analagous models. In educational administration training programs, the in-basket technique is often used to help students to apply theoretical learning when solving real problems. See *in-basket training*.

single salary schedule The most common type of schedule used to determine the salaries of American elementary and secondary teachers.

Under this schedule, teachers receive equivalent pay for equivalent training and experience irrespective of their professional effectiveness.

sinking fund See *debt service fund*.

site See *school site*.

site acquisition The process of choosing and securing title to real estate on which a building is likely to be erected.

situational determinants Conditions in the work environment that induce a leader to change certain aspects of his/her leadership behavior or cause a certain type of leader to emerge.

situational management See *contingency management*.

situational sensitivity The ability of a leader to perceive and gauge local situations and to adjust his/her leadership style accordingly. See *contingency management*.

skill acquisition curve See *learning curve*.

skills analysis Personnel process in which necessary job skills and the skills of incumbent employees are compared, with differences noted used as a way to ascertain training needs.

slack In the critical path systems approach to management, the difference between the earliest time and latest time in which a particular event can be completed. See *critical path method*.

slander A defamation that is spoken; a statement, communicated to a third party, that: (1) is false and malicious, and (2) injures one's reputation. See *libel*.

SMSA See *Standard Metropolitan Statistical Area*.

social promotion See *continuous promotion*.

social system A single organization that possesses an identity of its own. Social systems consist of subsystems which interact with each other, and normally do so in a manner that contributes to organizational stability. Individuals within the system carry out specific roles, these articulated with other roles. A school is an example of a social system.

social systems theory See *systems theory*.

software Programs, procedures, documents and other conceptual (nonmechanical) elements of a computer system; frequently contrasted with "hardware." See *hardware*.

sort Data processing term referring to the orderly arrangement of information, data, or digits.

sovereign immunity Somewhat outdated legal principle; holds that the sovereign (i.e., sovereign state) may not be sued without its consent. Applies to the U.S. and state governments; until 1960, applied to most boards of education as well. In recent years, numbers of states have modified or eliminated their immunity laws, frequently making jurisdictions liable for the actions for their employees. See *respondent superior*.

span of control An early concept of organization, less regarded today than it was in the past, suggesting that the optimum number of subordinate positions reporting to the same superior should be limited, usually no more than 5–8.

special assessment An other than regular levy against certain properties, the proceeds of which are used to pay for some specific improvement or service considered to benefit the property owner and community alike. Such levies are made by local governments (including fiscally independent boards of education).

special committee See *ad hoc committee*.

special education Generic term for instructional programs and services specially designed to meet the unique needs of exceptional children. According to Public Law 94-142, it includes classroom instruction, instruction in physical education, home instruction, and instruction in hospitals and institutions. See *exceptional child* and *Public Law 94-142*.

specialist teacher Or subject matter specialist, an instructor who teaches one or two academic subjects to more than one class of students during the course of a school day. Examples include English teacher, mathematics teacher, and physical education teacher. See *generalist teacher*.

specialized high school A secondary school that usually offers but one type of program. Its curriculum is designed for relatively homogeneous (sometimes preselected) students who have a major interest in common. Fine arts and vocational schools are examples of specialized high schools.

specific learning disability Category of special education students who have a disorder in one or more of the basic psychological processes involved in understanding or in using language (oral or written), which disorder may manifest itself in imperfect ability to listen, think, speak, read, write, spell, or do mathematical calculations. Examples include children with perceptual handicaps, brain injury, dyslexia, and developmental aphasia. Excludes children with learning problems resulting from visual, hearing, or motor handicaps; mental retardation; or environmental/cultural/economic disadvantage.

speech impaired Category of special education students with a communication disorder which affects the child's school performance adversely. Examples of such disorders include: stuttering, language impairment, impaired articulation, and voice impairment.

spiral curriculum Curriculum approach, conceptualized by Jerome Bruner, in which subject matter is prescribed and re-presented, following a simple-to-complex mode. Each re-presentation builds on learnings acquired earlier.

spot map Or pin map, a map containing colored pins or circles to indicate children's places of residency, with color codes used to distinguish different age groups (e.g., preschool, middle school). Such maps serve several purposes (e.g., to indicate pupil concentrations, to develop school bus routes, to help planners locate centrally-located school sites).

staff See *faculty*.

staff accounting Record-keeping activities having to do with employees of the school system. Included are related activities such as keeping personnel records current, filing, and information storage.

staff balance In personnel administration, the systematic recruitment and assignment of employees carried out in a manner guaranteeing that there is general evenness of personnel in terms of competence, load, sex, race, and ethnic origin, with the result that all students, regardless of building assignment, will enjoy equal educational opportunity.

staff development Personnel process designed to improve the personal and professional growth of teachers, supervisors, and administrators. In education, its basic goals are: (1) to improve instruction, and (2) to foster self-renewal among participants. The term is often used interchangeably with "inservice education." See *inservice education*.

staff relationship A form of organizational relationship frequently contrasted with "line relationship." Staff officers help line officers but are not part of the direct line showing chain of command. Their major functions are service, coordinative, and advisory. They derive their authority from technical knowledge. See *line relationship*.

staff retention rate A measure of employee holding power; more particularly, the percentage of employees remaining in the employ of a school system from one year to the next. The opposite of "staff separation rate." See *staff separation rate*.

staff separation rate The rate at which employees leave an organization during a period of time (typically one year); usually expressed as a percentage. Similar to "turnover." See *staff retention rate* and *turnover*.

staffing (1) In special education, an official meeting in which several concerned individuals (e.g., principal, teacher, counselor, parent) attempt to determine the appropriate placement/program for an exceptional child. (2) In personnel administration, activities related to the recruitment, selection, placement, retention, or retrenchment of employees.

standard deviation A statistical measure used to indicate how far scores fall from the mean of a distribution; a measure of dispersion, or "spread." The closer the scores are to the mean, the smaller is the standard deviation. When scores are normally distributed, approximately 68% lie within one deviation of the mean.

Standard Metropolitan Statistical Area (SMSA) A U.S. Bureau of the Census term for relatively large urban areas that: (1) transcend county and municipal boundaries, and (2) include at least one central city.

standardized test Carefully formulated and commercially published examination that is: (1) designed to yield a scientific sample of individual performance; (2) administered and scored in accordance with standardized procedures; and (3) accompanied by scientifically-developed norms to help with score interpretation.

standing committee A permanent committee that operates year after year.

stars Organizational members who operate at an outstanding level and are likely candidates for advancement within the organization.

state aid Financial assistance furnished to school districts by the states for the support of public education.

state board of education See *board of education, state.*

state department of education In each state, the agency responsible for monitoring education in accordance with law and the policies of its respective state board of education. (NOTE: Wisconsin is the only state that does not have a state board of education.) The departments carry out numerous functions (e.g., certification, school finance) and are headed by a chief state school officer. See *chief state school officer.*

state district A school district whose boundaries are coterminous with those of a state. Hawaii is the nation's only state district; Alaska, except for a few city and village districts, comes close to being a state district.

state education agency The organization charged with responsibility for overseeing public education in a state. A general term that normally includes: (1) the state board of education; (2) the chief state school officer; and (3) the state department of education staff.

state plan A written agreement between a state agency (e.g., state board of education) and a federal agency (e.g., U.S. Department of Education), formulated by the state, that indicates how the state will use/distribute federal funds allocated to it per federal law.

static equilibrium Systems theory term used to describe the condition that exists when an organization and/or its goals tend to maintain status quo in spite of environmental change(s) that may be taking place. Opposite of "dynamic equilibrium." See *dynamic equilibrium.*

status Position of an individual in a social system (e.g., teacher, student, principal). See *achieved status* and *ascribed status.*

status leader An appointed or elected leader (e.g., principal, superintendent, director); one who holds an official leadership title.

steward Or shop steward, a local union representative who carries out union duties among fellow employees. Some stewards are elected by their peers, others appointed by the union. In education, the steward may be known as a building or college representative.

stock insurance company An insurance company that is owned and controlled by its stockholders. Profits are distributed to stockholders in the form of dividends. See *mutual insurance company*.

store To enter and/or retain data in a computer; also, the part of a computer capable of receiving, retaining, and retrieving data.

storefront schools See *street academies*.

stores Supplies, materials, and equipment retained in central storerooms or warehouses and routinely requisitioned by authorized members of the school or school system.

straight life See *whole life insurance*.

strategy The means, method, or maneuver employed to bring about planned change.

street academies Early (1960's) alternative schools, frequently located in inner-city storefronts, that worked to meet the educational needs of dropouts or prospective dropouts; sometimes referred to as "storefront schools."

strike Work stoppage by a group of employees seeking to: (1) gain recognition; (2) improve working conditions; (3) resolve a dispute with management; or (4) express a grievance. The courts have defined a strike as a concerted refusal to work.

stroke A transactional analysis term for action taken by one person to recognize/commend another.

student accounting A system for collecting, recording, and analyzing information about students. In years past, this information related to students' records of attendance. Currently it contains other types of information and is used by counselors and others to help meet students' needs. (Also known as pupil accounting.)

student activities program Extracurricular or cocurricular activities, sponsored by the school, that meet the recreational, athletic, avocational, or leisure-time needs/interests of students. Examples of such activities are: (1) student newspaper; (2) dramatics; (3) band/orchestra/chorus; (4) photography club; and (5) baseball team.

student activity fund Or pupil activity fund, fund in which financial transactions related to school-sponsored student and inter-scholastic activities are recorded. Included are items such as proceeds from money-raising projects, locker fees, student organization memberships, and admissions receipts.

student body All students enrolled in a school or school system.

student capacity See *normal capacity*.

student code Printed set of rules and regulations for students, frequently formulated by students. Behaviors are normally expressed in positive terms. The code is also known as a student "code of ethics" or a student "code of behavior."

student council Student representatives, elected by the student body, who meet as a group to discuss selected school problems and to promote the general welfare of their school. Most councils are found operating in secondary schools; their faculty advisor is generally appointed by the principal.

student handbook Manual, prepared for use by students, that contains information about a school (e.g., student code of conduct, marking system).

student personnel services Generic term for student-support services offered by a school to assist students with their educational, personal, and social development. Examples of such services include guidance, placement assistance, information services, health services, and psychological services. Formerly referred to as "pupil personnel services."

student record See *educational record*.

student-teacher ratio See *pupil-teacher ratio*.

suboptimization Effort by an organizational subgroup to subordinate, even displace, the organization's goals to those of the subgroup; a parochial practice that inhibits organizational coordination.

suboptimum decision A less than satisfactory decision, one leading to other than desired outcome(s).

subordinate In organizations, one holding relatively lower rank, order, or status; an employee who reports to a superordinate (i.e., organizational superior).

substantive due process Assurance of equal treatment under the law; freedom from unfair or capricious action that deprives one of his/her constitutional right to life, liberty, or property. Derives from constitutional or statutory mandate. See *procedural due process*.

substitute bid See *alternate bid*.

subsystems Smaller and interdependent systems operating within, and as parts of a larger system. In a high school, for example, academic departments constitute subsystems of the school. See *system*.

subversive organization See *loyalty oath*.

summative evaluation Assessment of a program or project carried out after the program/project has been completed. See *formative evaluation*.

sunset budgeting See *zero-base budgeting*.

sunset legislation Laws that are automatically terminated at some predetermined time (e.g., after four years) unless reauthorized. Their purpose is to phase out programs or agencies no larger considered to be useful or satisfactory.

sunshine bargaining The carrying on of collective bargaining in meetings that are open to the public.

sunshine laws Federal and state legislation requiring public agencies (including school systems) to conduct open meetings (i.e., meetings open to the public). Provision is made for the conduct of closed (i.e., executive session) meetings for matters deemed to be confidential as in cases in which an individual's credit rating or sensitive business transactions are being discussed.

superintendent of schools The chief executive officer of a school system.

superordinate In organizations, one who is of higher rank; one's superior. In a school district, for example, the superintendent is a building principal's superordinate.

superseniority Special status sometimes accorded union officials that exempts them from regular layoff procedures during periods of retrenchment. Such special treatment is justified on the grounds that it serves to maintain stable relationships between management and labor.

supervision Processes and activities intended to improve an individual, a group, or a program. In education, supervision usually refers to activities that serve to improve the quality of teaching, learning, and curriculum. Such activities may be performed by any number of individuals such as a teacher, principal, consultant, director, or superintendent. See *developmental supervision* and *supervisor*.

supervision, clinical See *clinical supervision*.

supervision, instructional See *instructional supervision*.

supervisor One who supervises others. In education, the term is used both: (1) generically, and includes all personnel who render supervisory services (e.g., principal, department chair, assistant superintendent), and (2) specifically, to describe a particular and delimited leadership role (e.g., reading supervisor, supervisor of foreign language instruction). See *supervision*.

supply An item of a nonpermanent nature that is: (1) expendable, and (2) consumed, worn out, or deteriorated in use. Examples of school supplies are pencils, pads, and crayons.

supporting services Or support services, activities that serve to facilitate and enhance direct services. For example, through administrative, technical, and/or logistical "backstopping" by a school system's purchasing office (the supporting service), classroom instruction (the direct service) is performed more efficiently and/or effectively. See *direct services*.

supra-system A system's environment; the environment with which open systems interact. See *system*.

surety bond Written promise guaranteeing monetary compensation or indemnification in the event there is a failure on the part of those named in the document to perform specified acts (usually within a prescribed period of time).

surplus property Property, usually equipment items, no longer of use to the federal or state government. Such property, frequently in other than good condition, may be donated for authorized purposes (e.g., use in schools) or sold at low cost.

suspension, pupil Temporary separation of a student from school by an authorized school official (e.g., building principal) in accordance with established procedures. Such action is taken to encourage improved behavior or to emphasize the seriousness of an offense. Pupil suspensions are of four types: short-term, long-term, indefinite, and extracurricular.

syllabus The main points, or topical outline, of a course of study.

synectics A training method designed to stimulate creative thinking and problem-solving, usually by groups. Similar to brainstorming; developed by William J.J. Gordon.

synergy In organizations, the total energy which a group can command. "Maintenance synergy" and "effective synergy," terms coined by Raymond B. Cattell, distinguish between energy needed to sustain the organization (maintenance) and energy required to fulfill objectives (effective).

system (1) Organizational structure whose component parts (subsystems) work together for the purpose of achieving institutional goals. These parts interact with each other and their environment using standard operating procedures and environmental feedback. (2) In data processing, a synchronized collection of hardware and software.

system bargaining team See *negotiating team*.

systemic program Packaged or sequenced programs/activities designed to achieve some preconceived end. A textbook series, a specific instructional method, and programmed instruction are examples of systemic programs.

systems analysis A rational, step-by-step procedure for achieving tasks or solving problems which involves: (1) determining objectives and describing these using measurable terms; (2) identifying and sequencing the separate, yet interrelated steps to be followed—using logic, data, and analysis; (3) evaluation; and (4) revision if and as dictated by feedback. Systems analysis is one facet of the systems approach.

systems analyst An individual skilled in solving problems using a digital computer; an information systems specialist.

systems approach Generic term encompassing the several system-oriented processes/strategies employed by management. Systems analysis is one such process. Systems planning usually involves data collection, data analysis, formulation and implementation of action decisions, new data collection and analysis, and recycling of steps if and as deemed necessary.

systems design A conceptual representation indicating how, through use of the most efficient alternative/option, a particular goal is to be reached.

systems management Activities relating to monitoring the operation/progress of a system using preestablished criteria as bases for measurement.

systems theory Or general systems theory, an approach to the study of organizations which views organizations as total systems that: (1) are made up of numerous subsystems, each interacting with the others, and (2) in the case of so-called "open systems," concurrently interact with their respective environments.

T

tall organization A formal organization with a relatively large number of authority levels separating the lowest and highest level employees. Organizational distance between these two levels, measured hierarchically, is long, thus creating a "tall" table of organization. See *flat organization*.

tangible asset See *fixed asset*.

task A discrete unit of work assigned to or associated with a particular role. Some tasks are ad hoc in nature; others are performed continuously as a permanent job element.

task force An ad hoc group of individuals formed to carry out a specific organizational assignment (i.e., task).

tax Charge levied by a government to finance services to the public. See *income tax, progressive tax, property tax, regressive tax,* and *sales tax*.

tax anticipation notes A form of interim borrowing. Notes are issued in anticipation of yet-to-be collected tax revenues. The notes are repaid once the tax monies have been received, usually from the proceeds of the tax levy.

tax burden The proportion of personal or family income consumed by taxes.

tax limitations Tax ceilings, "caps," or "lids"; legal limits imposed on school districts and other governmental agencies for the purpose of restricting budget growth or tax increases, particularly the property tax. See *Proposition 13* and *Proposition 2½*.

tax rate The number of tax dollars to be paid by a property owner for each $100 of assessed valuation. When expressed in mills, the rate indicates the number of dollars to be paid for each $1.00 of assessed valuation. The tax rate for a school district is determined by dividing the total amount to be raised (levy) by the district's total assessed valuation.

taxonomy An orderly classification of data that have been grouped on the basis of their natural or logical relationships. In education, taxonomies of educational objectives have become well known in recent years and found useful for collecting/sorting facts and ideas.

Taxonomy of Educational Objectives System for classifying educational objectives, developed by Benjamin S. Bloom and others (1956), in which learning is divided into three major domains: affective, cognitive, and psychomotor. See *affective domain, cognitive domain,* and *psychomotor domain.*

teacher One who instructs. In public and some private schools, a person who is: (1) state certified, and (2) responsible for instructing and supervising students.

teacher aide A paraprofessional who assists a regular teacher by carrying out relatively routine assignments such as clerical work, operating audio-visual equipment, monitoring students, and working with small groups of pupils. Some aides are salaried; others volunteer their services.

teacher centers Federally or state supported sites whose principal function is to sponsor inservice training activities for teachers. Such centers may or may not involve university instructors, may or may not carry academic or inservice credit, and may or may not involve more than one school system. Centers differ from each other with respect to programs offered and approaches used.

teacher station See *teaching station.*

teaching machine Device for presenting programmed instruction to learners, usually on an individual basis. Features include: (1) a program; (2) a display mechanism (e.g., screen); (3) provision for student response to each stimulus item; and (4) instant feedback (i.e., "right" or "wrong").

teaching station Or teacher station, any room or facility in which a teacher offers instruction to students on a regular basis; includes spaces such as classrooms, gymnasia, and laboratories.

team administration Management concept requiring the active participation of all leaders, regardless of administrative level, in organizational planning and decision-making.

team teaching A form of instructional organization in which two or more teachers are responsible for planning and working together to provide instruction to one group of students. Some team teaching structures provide for differentiated staffing, an arrangement in which hierarchically different roles (e.g., master teacher, teacher, aide) are performed by team members.

technical education Instructional program that prepares students for occupations in specialized technological fields (e.g., electronics). Such programs are usually conducted at the post high school or adult levels.

technical skill One of three basic administrative skills (the others being "conceptual skill" and "human skill"). Technical skill refers to the competencies necessary to deal successfully with the procedures, techniques, and processes of management and education. See *conceptual skill* and *human skill*.

telecourse A full course of instruction taught via closed-circuit or broadcast television.

telelecture An arrangement that makes it possible for a teacher to lecture to students, though separated from them geographically, using telephone lines. Telelecture systems permit the lecturer to address several widely separated groups concurrently and frequently have a two-way communication capability (i.e., teacher-to-student and vice-versa).

temporary restraining order See *injunction*.

temporary system A short-term social system organized for the purpose of achieving some particular purpose and disbanded once that purpose has been realized. Examples of temporary systems are juries, conferences, ad hoc committees, training institutes, and scientific expeditions.

tenure The assurance of continuous employment granted to certain professional employees who have successfully completed a probationary period. Factors such as termination of a program or unsatisfactory job performance may bring about termination of tenure.

term In education, a scheduled component of the academic year (e.g., semester, quarter).

term bonds Bonds issued for a specified period of time. Interest only is paid during the specified time period; the entire principal is paid at the end of the term.

term insurance Life insurance that provides protection during the "term" of the policy. Death benefits are payable only if one dies during the term of years specified in the policy.

terminal (1) The point in a system or communication network at which information may enter or leave. (2) In data processing, an input-output device that permits man to exchange information with a machine.

terminal behavior Actual behavior exhibited by an individual following completion of a training program.

termination Involuntary separation from one's job. In education, it may be for "no fault" reasons such as declining enrollments or for "individual fault" reasons (e.g., unsatisfactory job performance).

test boring Pre-construction tests conducted to assess the load-bearing and subsoil qualities of land upon which a building is to be erected.

Tests of General Educational Development See *Certificate of High School Equivalency*.

T-group A small group of people that meets, usually with a trainer, for the purpose of improving members' interpersonal skills, work habits, motivation, and the like; often used as a synonym for *sensitivity training*.

Theil Coefficient School finance measure used to indicate variations in per-student expenditures or revenues. The larger the coefficient, the greater is the per-student deviation from zero. (A zero coefficient indicates perfect equality.)

theory A formal statement describing behavioral relationships among phenomena, set forth in the form of hypotheses, principles, and/or assumptions. Theoretical models derived from such statements provide a framework (i.e., guide) for research. Once a theory's hypotheses have been affirmed, and their predictive value established, the theory becomes a law.

Theory X One of two related theories developed by Douglas MacGregor (the other is "Theory Y"). Theory X assumes that: the average human being: (1) dislikes work, and avoids it when possible; (2) must be coerced to work toward realization of organization goals; and (3) lacks initiative, preferring to be directed and to assume as little responsibility as possible. See *Theory Y*.

Theory Y The second of two related theories developed by Douglas MacGregor; the opposite of "Theory X." Theory Y assumes that: (1) workers view physical and mental work as being natural; (2) they do not need to be coerced to work toward organizational goals; (3) individuals are ingenious, derive satisfaction from their work, and frequently seek out responsibility; and (4) human potential is poorly utilized by management. See *Theory X*.

Theory Z Title of a book by William Ouchi (1981) that describes a purportedly unique management style that carries the "Theory Z" name and is used by certain Japanese corporation managers. The Theory Z approach, Ouchi reports, emphasizes cooperative planning and decision-making by workers and managers, lifetime employment of workers, strong worker-manager loyalty, and the development of a positive work ethic.

therblig Term coined by Frank Gilbreth (reversal of his last name). A code word used in time and motion studies to describe any of 18 specific movements and mental efforts (e.g., grasp, inspect, handle).

thrust One of four "principal behavior" dimensions (subtests) included in the OCDQ. The term describes the principal who: (1) works to "move the organization," and (2) attempts to motivate his/her staff through personal example. See *Organizational Climate Description Questionnaire*.

time deposit A savings account that earns interest.

time management Arranging one's time such that important (i.e., high priority) goals are realized. Time management involves activities such as goal-setting, establishing work schedules, self-assessment viz-à-viz efficient use of time, striving for effective meetings, and the controlling of interruptions.

time-on-task In teaching, the number of minutes per day that an individual learner is actively working on instructional tasks. Also known as "academic learning time."

time-sharing A data processing arrangement that permits several operators, using remote terminals, to use a computer at the same time.

time sheet Or "job sheet," a form on which an employee lists different jobs performed and also records the amount of time devoted to each.

Title IX Commonly used reference to Title IX of Public Law 92–318 (Education Amendments of 1972), federal legislation that prohibits sexual discrimination in the admission/treatment of students. Several specific areas of possible discrimination are cited: (1) athletics; (2) financial assistance; (3) use of facilities; (4) access to courses; and (5) admissions.

tort A civil wrong, done by one person to another, for which a court may award damages. A wrong committed against one's person or property. Examples of tort are slander, negligence, and battery. See *assault, battery, negligence,* and *slander.*

total staff concept The idea that the quality, weaknesses, needs, etc. of the educational program are determined by characteristics of the total staff. Thus, personnel improvement programs, when planned, focus on improving total staff performance.

town/township districts School districts whose boundaries are coterminous with those of towns or townships. Such districts are found in New England, New Jersey, Pennsylvania, and Indiana.

tracking Or track system, the division of the instructional program into three levels (generally) to accommodate the different learning abilities of superior, average, and below average pupils. Used most frequently at the secondary school level.

training Occupational instruction. More particularly, special instruction designed to improve skills and/or to change job behavior. Such training may also include adult basic education, prevocational instruction, and refresher work.

trait A personal attribute (e.g., weight, intelligence, patience) possessed by all members of a population, but not in equal amounts.

trait rating Relatively subjective system of evaluating individual employees on the basis of certain personal characteristics (e.g., initiative, cooperation, intelligence, dependability).

trait theory of leadership Concept that leadership effectiveness correlates positively with selected personal traits such as the leader's intelligence, physical size, imagination, and persistence. Little evidence exists to corroborate the leadership capacity-traits relationship.

transaction In school business administration, any activity that alters the school system's financial condition.

transactional leadership style One of three ("transactional," "idiographic," "nomothetic") leadership style descriptions described by Egon Guba and Jacob Getzels. The transactional leader employs both idiographic and nomothetic styles, applying these selectively to individual situations. The needs of the organization and those of its members are integrated to the extent that circumstances permit. See *idiographic leadership style* and *nomothetic leadership style*.

transcript Document listing all courses attempted by a student, together with grades received and diplomas/degrees conferred. It becomes an official record when signed by a registrar or other institutional official and the seal of the institution has been affixed. The marking scale used by the issuing institution is frequently made a part of the transcript.

transfer The relocation, usually laterally, of an employee or student from one position/class/school to another, inside or outside an organization.

transfer voucher A voucher authorizing the transfer of funds or other resources from one fund/account to another. See *voucher*.

trend analysis A technique used to project future events on the basis of slopes in mathematical curves.

trial See *hearing*.

trial balance An accounting term used in conjunction with double-entry bookkeeping. All debit and credit items are checked to insure that the totals of the former are equal to those of the latter.

trial promotion Provisional promotion for students whose academic achievement has been questionable or less than satisfactory. Students are advanced to the next academic level on a trial basis; unsuccessful academic performance results in return to their former grade level.

trilateralism The introduction of a third party to arbitrate and mediate disagreements that two disputing parties are unable to resolve by themselves.

truancy Failure of a student to: (1) attend school regularly as prescribed by law, and (2) provide a reasonable excuse for such absence(s); willful, extended, unexcused absence.

truant officer See *attendance officer*.

true value Or true market value, the economic value of an asset (e.g., home, land) were it to be sold.

Trump Plan Organizational plan carrying the name of its developer, J. Lloyd Trump, that substituted large group, small group, and individualized instruction, flexibly scheduled, for the traditional secondary school "class" arrangement in which a subject specialist teaches 25–30 students on a fixed-schedule basis.

truncated high school See *incomplete high school*.

trusteeship In unions, action taken by a national or international union to take over control of a union local. Such action may be taken when serious mismanagement at the local level becomes apparent, illegal procedures at the local level are detected, or the local unit is considered to be in serious need of strengthening.

tuition Payment/charge for instruction.

turnover Changes in the roster of employees. More specifically, the number of individuals separated from an organization during a given period of time. See *staff retention rate*.

Type A lunch Classification used by the Department of Agriculture to describe the basic (and required) school lunch components. These are: (1) meat or meat alternate; (2) vegetable or fruit; (3) bread or bread alternate; and (4) milk. Recommended quantities vary with school level (e.g., preschool, Grades K–3).

U

UCEA See *University Council for Educational Administration*.

underwriter The individual or agency that purchases an entire new issue (e.g., school bond) and thereafter sells this security to the general public.

unfair labor practice Action by an employer or employee labor organization that violates the terms of the National Labor Relations Act or any of its counterpart state statutes. Examples of violations by management include: (1) refusal to engage in collective bargaining; (2) discouraging employees from joining a labor organization; and (3) restraining employees in the exercise of their lawful rights.

ungraded primary plan See *nongraded school plan* and *nongrading*.

ungraded school See *nongraded school plan* and *nongrading*.

unified district A school district that consists of both elementary and secondary schools. All grades (usually K–12) are governed by one board of education.

union shop Part of a collective bargaining agreement which specifies that all employees are to: (1) become union members soon after they are employed or after the agreement has been consummated, and (2) maintain their union membership as a condition of employment. Union shops are illegal in states with "right-to-work" laws.

unique decisions One-of-a-kind decisions for which little precedent and few, if any, guidelines exist. The resolution of unique problems requires creative decision-making. The "generic decision" vs. "unique decision" typology was developed by Peter F. Drucker. See *generic decisions*.

unit Subdivision of an organization (e.g., department).

unit cost In cost accounting, the cost of a particular unit of a good or service (e.g., cost per hundred, cost per hour).

unit executive control Term used to describe organizations headed by one chief executive (e.g., superintendent of schools) as distinct from "dual executive control" organizations (i.e., those with two chief executives who are equal in rank). See *dual executive control*.

unity of command A management principle, proffered by Henri Fayol, prescribing that no member of a formal organization should report to or receive direction from more than one superior.

unity of direction One of Henri Fayol's several management principles. Unity of direction suggests that there should be but one head and one plan for activities having the same objective.

University Council for Educational Administration (UCEA) Organization of American and Canadian universities that offer strong doctoral programs in educational administration. Membership is institutional. UCEA publishes a newsletter, research reports, *Educational Administration Abstracts*, *Educational Administration Quarterly*, and the *Journal of Educational Equity and Leadership*.

unregistered bond See *registered bond*.

unsecured bond Or debenture, a bond that is not backed by an asset.

unstructured day See *integrated day*.

upper division In colleges and universities, the third and fourth (i.e., junior and senior) years of a baccalaureate program. See *lower division*.

upward mobiles One of three classes of employees who exhibit certain common behaviors relating to ambition. According to Robert Presthus, creator of the term, upward mobiles: (1) identify closely with their organization and its leaders; (2) tend to be compliant, hence not change-prone; (3) exhibit high levels of job satisfaction; and (4) are likely to share in the rewards of their organization, including promotion. See *ambivalents* and *indifferents*.

urban school Literally, a school located within a city or densely populated area. In recent years, the term has come to be used as a euphemism for schools enrolling large ratios of poor, disadvantaged, and/or minority students.

V

validity The degree to which a test measures what it is supposed to measure, or the extent to which a test does what it was intended to do.

value added tax (VAT) Tax levied on a product or service during the various stages of its development; an indirect tax.

values clarification Instructional strategies that encourage students to formulate, express, and/or clarify their personal values relative to different topics or issues.

vandalism Wilfull destruction or defacing of property without the consent of the owner or the owner's agent. School vandalism refers to destruction, damages, loss, or defacement of a school building and/or its contents.

variable schedule A schedule for high school students in which class meeting days, length of class periods, and/or special activity periods are not uniform from one day to the next.

vendee The buyer in a sale.

vendor The seller in a sale.

vertical articulation The coordination of activities and/or programs from one level to another. Common examples in education are the efforts to achieve smooth instructional transitions from elementary to middle school, middle school to high school, and high school to college. The purpose, in these instances, is to bring about meaningful longitudinal programs with a minimum of gaps or duplication. See *articulation* and *horizontal articulation*.

vertical organization A method of classifying (i.e., organizing) students in a school in a manner that permits them to advance normally from one grade level to the next higher grade level, from the time of entry until departure.

vested authority Institutional (nomothetic) authority that is granted to a leader. Subordinates comply in accordance with their respective roles. See *entrusted authority*.

vested right In pension plans, a guarantee that an employee will not lose his/her pension rights if employment is terminated before he/she reaches retirement age. To qualify for retirement benefits, the employee must meet prescribed conditions such as: (1) minimum age (e.g., 60), and (2) years of service (e.g., 10). The pension may begin once minimum retirement age is reached.

veterans' preference Special and preferential hiring treatment accorded to veterans of the U.S. armed forces.

visually handicapped Category of special education students who are: (1) either blind or partially seeing, and (2) require special educational services for successful education.

vocational education A field of training that prepares one for the world of work (i.e., skilled, semi-skilled trades or occupations). Such programs normally include eight occupational areas: agriculture, distributive, health, occupational home economics, office occupations, technical, trade and industry, and vocational consumer/homemaking education.

voluntarism Practice of utilizing creative and other types of human resources, usually local, that are available to school systems and other governmental agencies on a no-cost basis. Examples include special study groups taught by local experts and volunteer tutors.

voucher In business administration, a document that: (1) authorizes the payment of money, and (2) usually indicates the account to which such expenditure is to be charged.

voucher system (1) Controversial plan for providing indirect financial support to elementary and secondary schools, public and private.

Certificates (vouchers) are issued to parents of school-aged children. Parents enroll their child(ren) in a school of their choice. Vouchers, presented to school officials, are subsequently forwarded to the government and redeemed for cash. (2) In accounting, a cash control system which requires that all expenditures be verified and approved before payments can be made.

vouchers payable Vouchers that have been approved but have yet to be paid. See *voucher*.

W

wage structure A schedule that indicates pay levels of different employee classifications (e.g., salaries paid to aides, teachers, principals).

warrant Order by a governmental body (e.g., school board), or one of its authorized officers, directing its treasurer to pay a specified amount to the person named or to the bearer. The warrant becomes a check, payable by a bank, once the treasurer's name has been affixed.

weighted pupil measures A system of apportioning state aid to school districts based on the recognition that it costs more to educate some pupils than others. For example, if the Grades 4–6 weighting is 1.0, it might be 1.33 for secondary students, 0.5 for half-day Kindergarteners, or 1.60 for the visually impaired.

Western Electric studies See *Hawthorne studies*.

wheel network A type of communication system that has been likened to a wheel. In such systems, one individual (the "hub") serves as the communication center for all others in the group/organization.

white flight The out-migration of white families from urban to suburban areas, a movement attributed to increased in-migration of minority groups into the cities.

whole life insurance Insurance that provides protection for as long as the policyholder lives; premiums remain constant. Also known as "straight life" and "ordinary life."

Winnetka Plan A plan for organizing elementary schools, introduced into the Winnetka, Illinois schools (1919) by Superintendent Carleton Washburne. Curriculum was divided into two parts: (1) basic skills, taught on an individualized and self-paced basis, and (2) cultural and creative learnings, taught in group settings.

withdrawal A student whose name is removed from the official roster of class or school members. Reasons for withdrawal include: (1) transfer; (2) dropping out; or (3) death.

withholding The practice of deducting from an employee's salary certain dollar amounts, prescribed by law, that represent his/her estimated federal, state, and/or city income tax.

word processing Using the microcomputer as a typewriter for the preparation, editing, storage, copying, and printing of written matter.

work load The amount of work which an individual employee or an organizational unit is expected to accomplish within a prescribed period of time.

work order An official request/instruction authorizing and directing completion of a particular work activity (e.g., partitioning an office). The order normally indicates: (1) description of job to be completed; (2) specifications; and (3) job number assigned.

work stoppage Temporary cessation of work, initiated by employees or the employer. Generic term that includes "strikes" and "lockouts"; a strategy sometimes used by groups of employees to resolve bargaining impasses or to register a protest.

work study program A school program that provides employment for students who, for financial reasons and without such job support, might not be able to remain in school.

working conditions All aspects of a worker's employment environment; does not normally include compensation, fringe benefits, or working hours.

workmen's compensation Payments to workers or their families for injuries or illnesses that are job-related. Workmen's compensation programs are governed by state laws and cover all employees (not independent contractors), including teachers, even if the employer may not have contributed to the injury or illness.

workshop Seminar, discussion group, etc. in which participants exchange ideas, demonstrate techniques, prepare materials/curricula; also a forum for group problem solving.

written agreement See *collective bargaining agreement*.

X–Y–Z

year-round school A school whose school year has been extended (usually to 12 months). Various scheduling approaches to implementing the year-round program have been developed. See *four- quarter plan, 45-15 plan,* and *quinmester plan.*

yellow dog contract Agreement between a worker and management indicating that, as a condition of employment, an individual is not a union member and that he/she must remain a nonmember. A term coined by unions.

zero-base budgeting A planning and budgeting process requiring the administrator of a "decision unit" (i.e., the organizational entity) to: (1) initiate his/her budget "from scratch"; (2) describe and justify each activity; and (3) present activity requests as "decision packages" (i.e., the concise documents prepared by each "decision unit").

zero reject Method of expressing the idea that no handicapped child shall be denied access to a free and appropriate public education.

zone of indifference Term coined by Chester Barnard to describe that range (zone) of orders from an organizational superior that the subordinate accepts without conscious questioning. The area's size varies from individual to individual; is frequently influenced by the individual's perception of his/her own job analysis.

BIBLIOGRAPHY

AECT Task Force on Definition and Terminology, *Educational Technology: A Glossary of Terms,* Washington, DC: Association for Educational Communication and Technology, 1979

Alexander, William F. and George, Paul S., *The Exemplary Middle School,* New York: Holt, Rinehart and Winston, Inc., 1981

Ammer, Christine and Ammer, Dean, *Dictionary of Business and Economics,* New York: The Free Press, 1977

American Association of School Administrators, *EDP and the School Administrator,* Washington, DC: The Association, 1967

American Association of School Administrators, *School District Organization,* Washington, DC: The Association, 1958

Anderson, Lester W. and Van Dyke, Lauren A., *Secondary School Administration* (Second Edition), Boston: Houghton Mifflin Company, 1972

Aquila, Frank D., *Title IX: Implications for Education of Women* (Fastback #156), Bloomington, IN: The Phi Delta Kappa Educational Foundation, 1981

Armstrong, David, et al., *Education: An Introduction,* New York: Macmillan Publishing Company, 1981

ASCD Curriculum Update (March 1982)

Augenblick, John, *School Finance Reform in the States: 1979,* Denver, CO: Education Commission of the States, July 1979

Baker, Stanley B., *School Counselor's Handbook: A Guide for Professional Growth and Development,* Boston: Allyn and Bacon, Inc., 1981

Ballentine, James A., *Ballentine's Law Dictionary* (Third Edition), Rochester, NY: Lawyers Co-operative Publishing Co., 1969

Bander, Edward J., *Dictionary of Selected Legal Terms and Maxims* (Second Edition), Dobbs Ferry, NY: Oceana Publications, 1979

Banki, Ivan S., *Dictionary of Supervision and Management: Authoritative, Comprehensive,* Los Angeles: Systems Research, 1976

Barnard, Chester I., *The Functions of the Executive,* Cambridge, MA: Harvard University Press, 1962

Beach, Dale S., *Personnel: The Management of People at Work* (Third Edition), New York: Macmillan Publishing Company, 1975

Beckham, Joseph, *Legal Implications of Minimum Competency Testing* (Fastback #138), Bloomington, IN: The Phi Delta Kappa Educational Foundation, 1980

Benson, Charles, *Equity in School Financing: Full State Funding* (Fastback #56), Bloomington, IN: The Phi Delta Kappa Educational Foundation, 1975

Benson, Charles and Shannon, Thomas A., *Schools Without Property Taxes: Hope or Illusion?* (Fastback #1), Bloomington, IN: The Phi Delta Kappa Educational Foundation, 1972

Black, Henry C., *Black's Law Dictionary* (Fourth Edition), St. Paul, MN: West Publishing Company, 1968

Blaschke, Charles, *Performance Contracting: Who Profits Most?* (Fastback #4), Bloomington, IN: The Phi Delta Kappa Educational Foundation, 1972

Boles, Harold, *Step by Step to Better School Facilities,* New York: Holt, Rinehart and Winston, Inc., 1965

Bolmeier, Edward C., *Legality of Student Disciplinary Practices,* Charlottesville, VA: The Michie Company, 1976

Bolmeier, Edward C., *Teachers' Legal Rights, Restraints and Liabilities,* Cincinnati, OH: W.H. Anderson Company, 1971

Bolton, Dale L., *Evaluating Administrative Personnel in School Systems,* New York: Teachers College Press, 1980

Bouvier, John, *Bouvier's Law Dictionary and Concise Encyclopedia* (Third Revision), St. Paul, MN: West Publishing Company, 1975

Broster, Eric J., *Glossary of Applied Management and Financial Statistics,* Epping, England: Gower Press, 1974

Brown, Warren B. and Moberg, Dennis J., *Organization Theory and Management: A Macro Approach,* New York: John Wiley and Sons, 1980

Byars, Lloyd L. and Rue, Leslie W., *Personnel Management: Concepts and Applications,* Philadelphia: W.B. Saunders Company, 1979

Campbell, Roald F. and Gregg, Russell (Editors), *Administrative Behavior in Education,* New York: Harper and Brothers Publishers, 1957

Campbell, Roald F., et al., *The Organization and Control of American Schools* (Fourth Edition), Columbus, OH: Charles E. Merrill Publishing Company, 1980

Candoli, I. Carl, et al., *School Business Administration: A Planning Approach* (Second Edition), Boston: Allyn and Bacon, Inc., 1978

Casey, Leo M., *School Business Administration,* New York: Center for Applied Research in Education, 1964

Casserly, Michael, et al., *School Vandalism: Strategies for Prevention,* Lexington, MA: Lexington Books, 1980

Castaldi, Basil, *Creative Planning of Educational Facilities,* Chicago: Rand McNally and Company, 1969

Castaldi, Basil, *Educational Facilities: Planning, Remodeling, and Management,* Boston: Allyn and Bacon, Inc., 1977

Castetter, William B., *The Personnel Function in Educational Administration* (Third Edition), New York: Macmillan Publishing Company, 1981

Chase, Clinton, *Measurement for Educational Evaluation,* Reading, MA: Addison-Wesley Publishing Co., 1974

Bibliography 181

Cheek, Logan M., *Zero-Base Budgeting Comes of Age,* New York: American Management Association, 1977

Cogan, Morris L., *Clinical Supervision,* Boston: Houghton Mifflin Company, 1972

Colbert, Douglas A., *Data Processing Concepts,* New York: McGraw-Hill Book Company, 1968

Collison, Koder M., *The Developers' Dictionary and Handbook,* Lexington, MA: D.C. Heath and Company, 1974

Connors, Eugene T., *Student Discipline and the Law* (Fastback #121), Bloomington, IN: The Phi Delta Kappa Educational Foundation, 1979

Council for Exceptional Children, *Special Education Administrative Policies Manual,* Reston, VA: The Council, September 1977

Dale, Ernest, *Management: Theory and Practice* (Third Edition), New York: McGraw-Hill Book Company, 1973

Davids, Lewis E., *Dictionary of Insurance* (Fourth Edition), Totowa, NJ: Littlefield, Adams, and Company, 1974

Davis, Donald E. and Nickerson, Jr., Neal C., *Critical Issues in School Personnel Administration,* Chicago: Rand McNally and Company, 1968

Dearman, Nancy B. and Plisko, Valena W., National Center for Education Statistics, *The Condition of Education* (1979 Edition), Washington, DC: U.S. Government Printing Office, 1979

Dearman, Nancy B. and Plisko, Valena W., National Center for Education Statistics, *The Condition of Education* (1981 Edition), Washington, DC: U.S. Government Printing Office, 1981

Dearman, Nancy B. and Plisko, Valena W., National Center for Education Statistics, *The Condition of Education* (1982 Edition), Washington, DC: U.S. Government Printing Office, 1982

de Ferranti, Basil (Editor), *Living With the Computer,* London, England: Oxford University Press, 1971

Dejnozka, Edward L. and Kapel, David E., *American Educators' Encyclopedia,* Westport, CT: Greenwood Press, 1982

Department of Elementary School Principals, *Elementary School Organization: Purposes, Patterns, Perspective,* Washington, DC: National Education Association, 1961

DeRoche, Edward F., *An Administrator's Guide for Evaluating Programs and Personnel,* Boston: Allyn and Bacon, Inc., 1981

Dillion-Peterson, Betty, *Staff Development/Organization Development* (1981 Yearbook), Alexandria, VA: Association for Supervision and Curriculum Development, 1981

Downs, Jr., James C., *Principles of Real Estate Management* (Twelfth Edition), Chicago: Institute of Real Estate Management, 1980

Dressel, Paul, *Administrative Leadership: Effective and Responsive Decision Making in Higher Education,* San Francisco: Jossey-Bass Publishers, 1981

Dressler, Gary, *Organization Theory: Integrating Structure and Behavior,* Englewood Cliffs, NJ: Prentice-Hall, Inc., 1980

Du Brin, Andrew J., *Fundamentals of Organizational Behavior: An Applied Perspective,* New York: Pergamon Press, 1974

Du Brin, Andrew J., *Personnel and Human Resource Management,* New York: D. Van Nostrand Company, 1981

Dufay, Frank R., *Ungrading The Elementary School,* West Nyack, NY: Parker Publishing Company, 1966

Ebel, Robert L., *Essentials of Educational Measurement,* Englewood Cliffs, NJ: Prentice-Hall, Inc., 1972

Edelfelt, Roy A. (Editor), *Inservice Education: Demonstrating Local Programs,* Bellingham, WA: Western Washington University, 1978

Educational Research Service, *How to Get the Most From Your ERS Subscription,* Arlington, VA: The Service, 1980

Edwards, Newton, *The Courts and the Public Schools: The Legal Basis of School Organization and Administration* (Third Edition), Chicago: University of Chicago Press, 1971

Eisenstadt, S. N., "Bureaucracy, Bureaucratization, and Debureaucratization," *Administrative Science Quarterly,* December 1959

Elsbree, Willard, et al., *Elementary School Administration and Supervision* (Third Edition), New York: American Book Company, 1967

Emmet, Dorothy, *Rules, Roles, and Relations,* London, England: St. Martin's Press, 1966

Engelkes, James R. and Vandergoot, David, *Introduction to Counseling,* Boston: Houghton Mifflin Company, 1982

English, Horace B. and English, Ava C., *A Comprehensive Dictionary of Psychological and Psychoanalytical Terms: A Guide to Usage,* New York: McKay, 1958

Eysenck, Hans J., et al. (Editors), *Encyclopedia of Psychology* (Second Edition), New York: Seabury Press, 1979

Faber, Charles F. and Shearron, Gilbert F., *Elementary School Administration: Theory and Practice,* New York: Holt, Rinehart and Winston, Inc., 1970

Feingold, Carl, *Introduction to Data Processing,* Dubuque, IA: W.C. Brown Company, 1971

Ferner, Jack D., *Successful Time Management: A Self-Teaching Guide,* New York: John Wiley and Sons, 1980

Findley, Warren G. and Bryan, Miriam M., *The Pros and Cons of Ability Grouping* (Fastback #66), Bloomington, IN: The Phi Delta Kappa Educational Foundation, 1975

Fischer, Louis, et al., *Teachers and the Law,* New York: Longman, 1981

Flygare, Thomas J., *Collective Bargaining in the Public Schools* (Fastback #99), Bloomington, IN: The Phi Delta Kappa Educational Foundation, 1977

Flygare, Thomas J., *The Legal Rights of Teachers* (Fastback #83), Bloomington, IN: The Phi Delta Kappa Educational Foundation, 1976

Foshay, Arthur W., (Editor), *The Rand McNally Handbook of Education,* Chicago: Rand McNally and Company, 1963

French, Derek and Saward, Heather, *Dictionary of Management,* Epping, England: Gower Press, 1975

Frost, Joe L. (Editor), *Early Childhood Education Rediscovered: Readings,* New York: Holt, Rinehart and Winston, Inc., 1968

Galloway, Charles, *Silent Language in the Classroom* (Fastback #86), Bloomington, IN: The Phi Delta Kappa Educational Foundation, 1976

Gatti, Richard D. and Gatti, Daniel J., *Encyclopedic Dictionary of School Law,* West Nyack, NY: Parker Publishing Company, 1975

Gearhart, Bill R., *Special Education for the '80s,* St. Louis: The C. V. Mosby Company, 1980

Gerard, Harold J. and Miller, Norman, *School Desegregation: A Long-Term Study,* New York: Plenum Press, 1975

Getzels, Jacob W., et al., *Educational Administration as a Social Process: Theory, Research, Practice,* New York: Harper and Row, Publishers, 1968

Gibson, Janice T., *Psychology for the Classroom* (Second Edition), Englewood Cliffs, NJ: Prentice-Hall, Inc., 1980

Gibson, R. Oliver and Hunt, Herold, C., *The School Personnel Administrator,* Boston: Houghton Mifflin Company, 1965

Gilroy, Thomas P., *Educator's Guide to Collective Negotiations,* Columbus, OH: Charles E. Merrill Publishing Co., 1969

Glatthorn, Allan A., *Alternatives in Education: Schools and Programs,* New York: Dodd Mead, 1975

Glickman, Carl D., "The Developmental Approach to Supervision," *Educational Leadership,* November 1980

Goldhammer, Robert, *Clinical Supervision: Special Methods for the Supervision of Teachers,* New York: Holt, Rinehart and Winston, Inc., 1969

Good, Carter V. (Editor), *Dictionary of Education* (Third Edition), New York: McGraw-Hill Book Company, 1973

Gorton, Richard A., *School Administration: Challenge and Opportunity for Leadership,* Dubuque, IA: Wm. C. Brown Company, 1976

Gould, Julius and Kolb, William L. (Editors), *A Dictionary of the Social Sciences,* New York: The Free Press, 1964

Grady, Walteen, et al., *Sex Equity Ideabook for the District of Columbia Public Schools,* Washington, DC: Educational Equity Institute, The American University, July 1980

Grant, Carl A., *Community Participation in Education,* Boston: Allyn and Bacon, Inc., 1979

Greenhalgh, John, *Practitioner's Guide to School Business Management,* Boston: Allyn and Bacon, Inc., 1978

Griffiths, Daniel E. (Editor), *Behavioral Science and Educational Administration* (63rd National Society for the Study of Education Yearbook, Part II), Chicago: University of Chicago Press, 1964

Griffiths, Daniel E., et al., *Organizing Schools for Effective Education,* Danville, IL: The Interstate Printers and Publishers, 1962

Gurwitz, Aaron S., *The Economics of Public School Finance,* Cambridge, MA: Ballinger Publishing Company, 1982

Guthrie, James, *Equity in School Financing* (Fastback #57), Bloomington, IN: The Phi Delta Kappa Educational Foundation, 1975

Guthrie, James (Editor), *School Finance Policies and Practices* (First Annual Yearbook of the American Education Finance Association), Cambridge, MA: Ballinger Publishing Company, 1980

Hale, George E. and Palley, Marian L., *The Politics of Federal Grants,* Washington, DC: Congressional Quarterly Press, 1981

Hall, Francine S. and Albrecht, Maryann H., *The Management of Affirmative Action,* Santa Monica, CA: Goodyear Publishing Company, 1979

Halpin, Andrew W. and Croft, Don B., *The Organizational Climate of Schools,* Chicago: Midwest Administration Center, University of Chicago, 1963

Hanson, E. Mark, *Educational Administration and Organizational Behavior,* Boston: Allyn and Bacon, Inc., 1979

Harris, Ben M. and Bessent, Wailand (with McIntyre, Kenneth E.), *Inservice Education: A Guide to Better Practice,* Englewood Cliffs, NJ: Prentice-Hall, Inc., 1969

Harris, Ben M., et al., *Personnel Administration in Education: Leadership for Instructional Improvement,* Boston: Allyn and Bacon, Inc., 1979

Hasazi, Susan E., et al., *Mainstreaming: Merging Regular and Special Education* (Fastback #124), Bloomington, IN: The Phi Delta Kappa Educational Foundation, 1979

Hazard, William R., *Education and the Law: Cases and Materials on Public Schools,* New York: The Free Press, 1971

Heathers, Glen, *Organizing Schools Through the Dual Progress Plan: Tryouts of a New Plan for Elementary and Middle Schools,* Danville, IL: Interstate, 1967

Heimanson, Rudolph, *Dictionary of Political Science and Law,* Dobbs Ferry, NY: Oceana Publications, 1967

Hencley, Stephen P., et al., *The Elementary School Principalship,* New York: Dodd Mead, 1970

Hentschke, Guilbert C., *Management Operations in Education,* Berkeley, CA: McCutchan Publishing Corporation, 1975

Herman, Jerry J., *School Administrator's Accountability Manual: Tested Programs to Improve Your School's Effectiveness,* West Nyack, NY: Parker Publishing Company, 1979

Heyman, Mark, *Simulation Games For the Classroom* (Fastback #54), Bloomington, IN: The Phi Delta Kappa Educational Foundation, 1975

Hill, Joseph E., *How Schools Can Apply Systems Analysis* (Fastback #6), Bloomington, IN: The Phi Delta Kappa Educational Foundation, 1972

Horton, Paul B. and Hunt, Chester L., *Sociology* (Third Edition), New York: McGraw-Hill Book Company, 1972

Hoult, Thomas F., *Dictionary of Modern Sociology,* Totowa, NJ: Littlefield, Adams, and Company, 1969

Howe, Clifford E., *Administration of Special Education,* Denver, CO: Love Publishing Company, 1981

Hoy, Wayne K. and Miskel, Cecil G., *Educational Administration: Theory, Research, and Practice* (Second Edition), New York: Random House, 1982

Hughes, Helen M. (Editor), *Delinquents and Criminals: Their Social World,* Boston: Holbrook Press, May 1974

Hull, Keith A., "Computerized Education" in Mitzel, Harold E. (Editor), *Encyclopedia of Educational Research,* Volume I (Fifth Edition), New York: The Free Press, 1982

Ingalls, John D., *A Trainers Guide to Androgogy* (Revised Edition), U.S. Department of Health, Education, and Welfare, Washington, DC: U.S. Government Printing Office, May 1973

Jaffee, Cabot L. and Sefcik, Jr., Joseph T., "What Is an Assessment Center?," *Personnel Administrator,* February 1980

Jarvis, Oscar, et al., *Public School Business Administration and Finance: Effective Policies and Practices,* West Nyack, NY: Parker Publishing Company, 1967

Johannsen, Hano and Page, G. Terry, *International Dictionary of Management: A Practical Guide,* London, England: Kogan Page, 1975

Johannsen, Hano and Robertson, Andrew, *Management Glossary,* New York: American Elsevier Publishing Company, 1968

Johansen, John H., et al., *American Education: The Task of the Teacher,* Dubuque, IA: Wm. C. Brown Company Publishers, 1971

Johnson, George M., *Education Law,* East Lansing, MI: Michigan State University Press, 1969

Jones, James J., et al., *Secondary School Administration,* New York: McGraw-Hill Book Company, 1969

Jordan, K. Forbis and Cambron-McCabe, Nelda H. (Editors), *Perspectives in State School Support Programs* (Second Annual Yearbook of the American Education Finance Association), Cambridge, MA: Ballinger Publishing Company, 1981

Jordan, Thomas E., *America's Children: An Introduction to Education,* Chicago: Rand McNally and Company, 1973

Kast, Fremont E. and Rosenzweig, James E., *Organization and Management: A Systems Approach* (Third Edition), New York: McGraw-Hill Book Company, 1974

Katz, Daniel and Kahn, Robert L., *The Social Psychology of Organizations,* New York: John Wiley & Sons, 1966

Kaufman, Roger A., *Educational System Planning,* Englewood Cliffs, NJ: Prentice-Hall, Inc., 1972

Keim, Marianne T., *Running Press Glossary of Insurance Language,* Philadelphia: Running Press, 1978

Keith, Lyman A., *Accounting: A Management Perspective,* Englewood Cliffs, NJ: Prentice-Hall, Inc., 1980

Kelly, Leo and Vergason, Glenn A., *Dictionary of Special Education and Rehabilitation,* Denver, CO: Love Publishing Company, 1978

Kemerer, Frank R. and Deutsch, Kenneth L., *Constitutional Rights and Student Life: Value Conflict in Law and Education,* St. Paul, MN: West Publishing Company, 1979

Kemp, Roger L., *Coping With Proposition 13,* Lexington, MA: Lexington Books, 1980

Keyfitz, Nathan and Flieger, Wilhelm, *Population: Facts and Methods of Demography,* San Francisco: W.H. Freeman, 1971

Knezevich, Stephen J., *Administration of Public Education* (Second Edition), New York: Harper and Row, Publishers, 1969

Knowles, Asa S. (Editor), *The International Encyclopedia of Higher Education* (Volume I), San Francisco: Jossey-Bass Publishers, 1977

Kohler, Eric L., *A Dictionary for Accountants* (Fifth Edition), Englewood Cliffs, NJ: Prentice-Hall, Inc., 1975

Kowalski, Theodore J., "Attitudes of School Principals Toward Decentralized Budgeting," *Journal of Education Finance,* Summer 1980

Landers, Thomas J. and Myers, Judith G., *Essentials of School Management,* Philadelphia: W.B. Saunders Company, 1977

Leggett, Stanton, et al., *Planning Flexible Learning Places,* New York: McGraw-Hill Book Company, 1977

Levy, Michael H., *A Handbook of Personal Insurance Terminology,* Lynbrook, NY: Farnsworth Publishing Company, 1968

Lewis, Jr., James, *School Management by Objectives,* West Nyack, NY: Parker Publishing Company, 1974

Lieberman, Ann and McLaughlin, Milbrey W. (Editors), *Policy Making in Education* (81st Yearbook of the National Society for the Study of Education, Part I), Chicago: University of Chicago Press, 1982

Lieberman, Myron and Moskow, Michael H., *Collective Negotiations for Teachers: An Approach to School Administration,* Chicago: Rand McNally and Company, 1966

Lipham, James M. and Hoeh, Jr., James A., *The Principalship: Foundations and Functions,* New York: Harper and Row, Publishers, 1974

Lucio, William H. and McNeil, John D., *Supervision in Thought and Action* (Third Edition), New York: McGraw-Hill Book Company, 1979

Luthans, Fred and Martinko, Mark J., *The Practice of Supervision and Management,* New York: McGraw-Hill Book Company, 1979

Matulich, Serge and Heitger, Lester E., *Financial Accounting,* New York: McGraw-Hill Book Company, 1980

McAshan, H. H., *Writing Behavioral Objectives: A New Approach,* New York: Harper and Row, Publishers, 1970

McCarthy, Martha M. and Cambron, Nelda H., *Public School Law: Teachers' and Students' Rights,* Boston: Allyn and Bacon, Inc., 1981

McGlasson, Maurice, *The Middle School: Whence? What? Whither?* (Fastback #22), Bloomington, IN: The Phi Delta Kappa Educational Foundation, 1973

McGrath, J. H., *Planning Systems for School Executives: The Unity of Theory and Practice,* Scranton, PA: Intext Educational Publishers, 1972

McGraw-Hill Dictionary of Modern Economics: A Handbook of Terms and Organizations (Second Edition), New York: McGraw-Hill Book Company, 1973

McManama, John, *Systems Analysis for Effective School Administration,* West Nyack, NY: Parker Publishing Company, 1971

McMillan, Charles B., *Magnet Schools: An Approach to Voluntary Desegregation* (Fastback #141), Bloomington, IN: The Phi Delta Kappa Educational Foundation, 1980

Meers, Gary D. (Editor), *Handbook of Special Vocational Needs Education,* Rockville, MD: Aspen Systems Corporation, 1980

Mehrens, William A. and Lehmann, Irvin J., *Measurement and Evaluation in Education and Psychology,* New York: Holt, Rinehart and Winston, Inc., 1973

Meranto, Philip, *School Politics in the Metropolis,* Columbus, OH: Charles E. Merrill Publishing Company, 1970

Metcalf, Richard W. and Tidard, Pierre L., *Introduction to Accounting,* Philadelphia: W.B. Saunders Company, 1975

Miles, Matthew (Editor), *Innovation in Education,* New York: Bureau of Publications, Teachers College, Columbia University, 1964

Miller, Van, et al., *The Public Administration of American School Systems* (Second Edition), New York: Macmillan Publishing Company, 1972

Miller, William C. and Newbury, David N., *Teacher Negotiations: A Guide for Bargaining Teams,* West Nyack, NY: Parker Publishing Company, 1970

Miscallef, Benjamin A., *An Introduction to Data Processing,* Menlo Park, CA: Cummings Publishing Co., 1971

Mitchell, G. Duncan, *A Dictionary of Sociology,* Chicago: Aldine Publishing Company, 1968

Moehlman, Arthur B., *School Administration: Its Development, Principles, and Functions in the United States* (Second Edition), Boston: Houghton Mifflin Company, 1951

Morgan, Edward P., "The Effects of Proposition 2½ in Massachusetts," *Phi Delta Kappan,* December 1982

Moss, Julie M. (Editor), *Ayer Glossary of Advertising and Related Terms* (Second Edition), Philadelphia: Ayer Press, 1977

National Association of Insurance Commissioners, "Life Insurance Buyer's Guide" (a brochure), Philadelphia Life Insurance Company, February 1977

National Center for Education Statistics, *Combined Glossary: Terms and Definitions from the Handbooks of the State Educational Records and Reports Series,* Washington, DC: U.S. Government Printing Office, 1974

National Center for Education Statistics, *Educational Technology: A Handbook of Standard Terminology and a Guide for Recording and Reporting Information about Educational Technology* (Handbook X), Washington, DC: U.S. Government Printing Office, 1975

National Center for Education Statistics, *Property Accounting: A Handbook of Standard Terminology and a Guide for Classifying Information About Education Property* (Handbook III, Revised), Washington, DC: U.S. Government Printing Office, 1977

National Education Association, "National Education Association: A Brief Description" (a brochure), Washington, DC: The Association, June 1976

National Institute of Education, *How to Use ERIC,* Washington, DC: U.S. Government Printing Office, undated

Neagley, Ross L. and Evans, Dean N., *Handbook for Effective Supervision* (Third Edition), Englewood Cliffs, NJ: Prentice-Hall, Inc., 1980

Newell, Clarence A., *Human Behavior in Educational Administration,* Englewood Cliffs, NJ: Prentice-Hall, Inc., 1978

Nigro, Felix A. and Nigro, Lloyd G., *Modern Public Administration* (Fourth Edition), New York: Harper and Row, Publishers, 1977

Noll, Victor H. and Scannell, Dale P., *Introduction to Educational Measurement* (Third Edition), New York: Houghton Mifflin Company, 1972

Nyquist, Ewald B. and Hawes, Gene R. (Editors), *Open Education: A Sourcebook for Parents and Teachers,* New York: Bantam Books, 1972

O'Brien, James A., *Computers in Business Management: An Introduction* (Revised Edition), Homewood, IL: Richard D. Irwin, 1979

Ostrander, Kenneth H., *A Grievance Arbitration Guide for Educators*, Boston: Allyn and Bacon, Inc., 1981

Otto, Henry J. and Sanders, David C., *Elementary School Organization and Administration* (Fourth Edition), New York: Appleton-Century-Crofts, Inc., 1964

Ouchi, William G., *Theory Z*, Reading, MA: Addison-Wesley, 1981

Ovard, Glen F., *Administration of the Changing Secondary School*, New York: Macmillan Publishing Company, 1966

Owens, Robert G., *Organizational Behavior in Education* (Second Edition), Englewood Cliffs, NJ: Prentice-Hall, Inc., 1981

Owens, Robert G., *Organizational Behavior in Schools*, Englewood Cliffs, NJ: Prentice-Hall, Inc., 1970

Passow, A. Harry (Editor), *Reaching the Disadvantaged Learner*, New York: Teachers College Press, 1970

Peterson, Leroy, et al., *The Law and Public School Operation* (Second Edition), New York: Harper and Row, Publishers, 1978

Pfeiffer, J. William and Jones, John E., *The 1980 Annual Handbook for Group Facilitators*, San Diego, CA: University Associates, 1980

Phi Delta Kappa, "Introduction to Phi Delta Kappa" (a brochure), Bloomington, IN: Phi Delta Kappa, February 1979

Phi Delta Kappa, "Practical Applications of Research" (a brochure), June 1981

Presthus, Robert, *The Organizational Society: An Analysis and a Theory*, New York: Alfred A. Knopf, 1962

Public Law 93-380, *United States Statutes at Large* (Volume 88, Part I), Washington, DC: U.S. Government Printing Office, 1976

Public Law 94-142, *United States Statutes at Large* (Volume 89), Washington, DC: U.S. Government Printing Office, 1977

Putnam, John F., National Center for Education Statistics, *Student/Pupil Accounting: Standard Terminology and Guide for Managing Student Data in Elementary and Secondary Schools, Community/Junior Colleges, and Adult Education* (Handbook V, Revised 1974), Washington, DC: U.S. Government Printing Office, 1974

Reavis, Charles A., *Teacher Improvement Through Clinical Supervision* (Fastback #111), Bloomington, IN: The Phi Delta Kappa Educational Foundation, 1978

Reeves, Charles E., *School Boards: Their Status, Functions and Activities*, Westport, CT: Greenwood Press (reprinted), 1969

Regier, Herold, *Too Many Teachers: Fact or Fiction?* (Fastback #5), Bloomington, IN: The Phi Delta Kappa Educational Foundation, 1972

Reutter, E. and Hamilton, R., *The Law of Public Education* (Second Edition), Mineola, NY: The Foundation Press, 1976

Richey, Robert W., *Planning for Teaching: An Introduction to Education* (Fourth Edition), New York: McGraw-Hill Book Company, 1968

Riegel, Rodney P. and Lovell, Ned B., *Minimum Competency Testing* (Fastback #137), Bloomington, IN: The Phi Delta Kappa Educational Foundation, 1980

Roberts, Geoffrey K., *A Dictionary of Political Analysis*, London, England: Longman, 1971
Robinson, William N., *American Education: Its Organization and Control*, Columbus, OH: Charles E. Merrill Publishing Company, 1968
Rosenberg, Jerry M., *Dictionary of Business and Management*, New York: John Wiley and Sons, 1978
Sabatino, David A. and Miller, Ted L. (Editors), *Describing Learner Characteristics of Handicapped Children and Youth*, New York: Grune and Stratton,1979
Sadker, Myra P. and Sadker, David M., *Teachers Make the Difference: An Introduction to Education*, Cambridge, MA: Harper and Row, Publishers, 1980
St. John, Nancy H., *School Desegregation: Outcomes for Children*, New York: John Wiley and Sons, 1975
Selznick, Philip, "Foundations of the Theory of Organization," *American Sociological Review*, February 1948
"SERDACumentation: Newsletter of the Southeast Regional Data Center," Southeast Regional Data Center, Florida International University, May 1982
Sergiovanni, Thomas J., et al., *Educational Governance and Administration*, Englewood Cliffs, NJ: Prentice-Hall, Inc., 1980
Sergiovanni, Thomas J. and Carver, Fred D., *The New School Executive* (Second Edition), New York: Harper and Row, Publishers, 1980
Shafritz, Jay M., *Dictionary of Personnel Management and Labor Relations*, Oak Park, IL: Moore Publishing Company, 1980
Shuster, Albert H. and Stewart, Don H., *The Principal and the Autonomous Elementary School*, Columbus, OH: Charles E. Merrill Publishing Company, 1973
Silberman, Harry F. (Editor), *Education and Work* (81st Yearbook of the National Society for the Study of Education, Part II), Chicago: University of Chicago Press, 1982
Simon, Herbert A., *Administrative Behavior: A Study of Decision-Making Processes in Administrative Organization* (Third Edition), New York: The Free Press, 1976
Sladek, Frea E. and Stein, Eugene L., *Grant Budgeting and Finance: Getting the Most Out of Your Grant Dollar*, New York: Plenum Press, 1981
Slavin, Albert, et al., *Financial Accounting: A Basic Approach*, Hinsdale, IL: The Dryden Press, 1980
Smith, Robert M. and Neisworth, John T., *The Exceptional Child: A Functional Approach*, New York: McGraw-Hill Book Company, 1975
Smith, Vernon, et al., *Optional Alternative Public Schools* (Fastback #42), Bloomington, IN: The Phi Delta Kappa Educational Foundation, 1974
Snyder, Fred A., and Peterson, R. Duane, *Dynamics of Elementary School Administration*, Boston: Houghton Mifflin Company, 1970
Spencer, Donald D., *Introduction to Information Processing*, Columbus, OH: Merrill Publishing Company, 1974

Stanley, Julian C. and Hopkins, Kenneth D., *Educational and Psychological Measurement and Evaluation,* Englewood Cliffs, NJ: Prentice-Hall, Inc., 1972

Steele, Sara M., *Contemporary Approaches to Program Evaluation: Implications for Evaluating Programs for Disadvantaged Adults,* Syracuse, NY: ERIC Clearinghouse on Adult Education, 1973

Steers, Richard M. and Porter, Lyman W., *Motivation and Work Behavior* (Second Edition), New York: McGraw-Hill Book Company, 1979

Stern, Ralph D. (Editor), *The School Principal and the Law,* Topeka, KS: National Organization on Legal Problems of Education, 1980

Stogdill, Ralph M., *Handbook of Leadership: A Survey of Theory and Research,* New York: The Free Press, 1974

Stoops, Emery, et al., *Handbook of Educational Administration: A Guide for the Practitioner,* Boston: Allyn and Bacon, Inc., 1975

Stoops, Emery and Johnson, Russell E., *Elementary School Administration,* New York: McGraw-Hill Book Company, 1967

Stratemeyer, Florence B., et al., *Developing a Curriculum for Modern Living* (Second Edition), New York: Teachers College, Columbia University, 1957

Strevell, Wallace H. and Burke, Arvid J., *Administration of the School Building Program,* New York: McGraw-Hill Book Company, 1959

Supplee, Charles B., "An Analysis of Factors in Interunit Management and Governance Influencing Impact of Teacher Corps Programs," unpublished doctoral dissertation, University of Nebraska, July 1978

Swezey, Robert W., *Individual Performance Assessment: An Approach to Criterion-Referenced Test Development,* Reston, VA: Reston Publishing Company, Inc., 1981

Tavel, David, *Church-State Issues in Education* (Fastback #123), Bloomington, IN: The Phi Delta Kappa Educational Foundation, 1979

Terry, George R., *A Guide to Management,* Homewood, IL: Learning System Company, 1981

Theodorson, George A. and Theodorson, Achilles G., *A Modern Dictionary of Sociology,* New York: Crowell, 1969

Tidwell, Sam B., *Financial and Managerial Accounting for Elementary and Secondary School Systems,* Chicago: The Research Corporation/Association of School Business Officials, 1974

Tronc, Keith E. (Editor), *Financial Management in School Administration,* St. Lucia, Australia: University of Queensland Press, 1977 (distributed by Prentice-Hall, Inc.)

Tuttle, Edward M., *School Board Leadership in America* (Revised), Chicago: Interstate Printers and Publishers, 1963

Twomley, Dale E., *Parochiaid and the Courts,* Berrien Springs, MI: Andrews University Press, 1979

Unruh, Glenys G. and Alexander, William M., *Innovations in Secondary Education* (Second Edition), New York: Holt, Rinehart and Winston, Inc., 1970

Valente, William D., *Law in the Schools,* Columbus, OH: Charles E. Merrill Publishing Company, 1980

Van Til, William, *Education: A Beginning,* Boston: Houghton Mifflin Company, 1971
Von Haden, Herbert I. and King, Jean Marie, *Innovations in Education: Their Pros and Cons,* Worthington, OH: Charles A. Jones Publishing Company, 1971
Webster, Staten W. (Editor), *The Disadvantaged Learner: Knowing, Understanding, Educating,* San Francisco: Chandler Publishing Company, 1966
Wiles, Jon and Bondi, Joseph, *Supervision: A Guide to Practice,* Columbus, OH: Charles E. Merrill Publishing Company, 1980
Worthen, Blaine R. and Sanders, James R., *Educational Evaluation: Theory and Practice,* Worthington, OH: Charles A. Jones Publishing Company, 1973

APPENDIXES

Appendix I

STATEMENT OF ETHICS FOR SCHOOL ADMINISTRATORS

An educational administrator's professional behavior must conform to an ethical code. The code must be idealistic and at the same time practical, so that it can apply reasonably to all educational administrators. The administrator acknowledges that the schools belong to the public they serve for the purpose of providing educational opportunities to all. However, the administrator assumes responsibility for providing professional leadership in the school and community. This responsibility requires the administrator to maintain standards of exemplary professional conduct. It must be recognized that the administrator's actions will be viewed and appraised by the community, professional associates, and students. To these ends, the administrator subscribes to the following statements of standards.

The educational administrator:

(1) Makes the well-being of students the fundamental value of all decision making and actions.
(2) Fulfills professional responsibilities with honesty and integrity.
(3) Supports the principle of due process and protects the civil and human rights of all individuals.
(4) Obeys local, state, and national laws and does not knowingly join or support organizations that advocate, directly or indirectly, the overthrow of the government.
(5) Implements the governing board of education's policies and administrative rules and regulations.
(6) Pursues appropriate measures to correct those laws, policies, and regulations that are not consistent with sound educational goals.

Reprinted with permission of the American Association of School Administrators

(7) Avoids using positions for personal gain through political, social, religious, economic, or other influence.

(8) Accepts academic degrees or professional certification only from duly accredited institutions.

(9) Maintains the standards and seeks to improve the effectiveness of the profession through research and continuing professional development.

(10) Honors all contracts until fulfillment, release or dissolution mutually agreed upon by all parties to contract.

───────────────────────────────── Appendix II
NATIONAL AND REGIONAL ORGANIZATIONS OF INTEREST TO EDUCATIONAL ADMINISTRATORS

AMERICAN ASSOCIATION OF SCHOOL ADMINISTRATORS
1801 North Moore Street
Arlington, VA 22209

AMERICAN ASSOCIATION OF SCHOOL PERSONNEL ADMINISTRATORS
6483 Tanglewood Lane
Seven Hills, OH 44131

AMERICAN EDUCATIONAL RESEARCH ASSOCIATION
1230 Seventeenth St., N.W.
Washington, DC 20036

AMERICAN FEDERATION OF SCHOOL ADMINISTRATORS, AFL/CIO
110 East 42nd Street
Suite 1510
New York, New York 10017

AMERICAN FEDERATION OF TEACHERS, AFL/CIO
11 Dupont Circle, N.W.
Washington, DC 20036

ASSOCIATION FOR SUPERVISION AND CURRICULUM DEVELOPMENT
225 North Washington Street
Alexandria, VA 22314

ASSOCIATION OF SCHOOL BUSINESS OFFICIALS
OF THE UNITED STATES AND CANADA
720 Garden Street
Park Ridge, IL 60068

Principal Source: Lois V. Lopez, Compiler, *Directory of Education Associations, 1980–81* (U.S. Department of Education) Washington, DC: U.S. Government Printing Office, 1981).

COUNCIL OF ADMINISTRATORS OF SPECIAL EDUCATION, INC.
6807 Park Heights Avenue
Baltimore, MD 21215

COUNCIL OF CHIEF STATE SCHOOL OFFICERS
379 Hall of the States
400 North Capital Street, N.W.
Washington, DC 20001

COUNCIL OF EDUCATIONAL FACILITY PLANNERS—
INTERNATIONAL
29 West Woodruff Avenue
Columbus, OH 43210

COUNTRY DAY SCHOOL HEADMASTERS' ASSOCIATION
Princeton Day School
P.O. Box 75
The Great Road
Princeton, NJ 08540

HEADMASTERS ASSOCIATION
Harvard School
3700 Coldwater Canyon Road
North Hollywood, CA 91604

NATIONAL ALLIANCE OF BLACK SCHOOL EDUCATORS
1401 14th Street, N.W.
Washington, DC 20005

NATIONAL ASSOCIATION OF ELEMENTARY SCHOOL PRINCIPALS
1920 Association Drive
Reston, VA 22091

NATIONAL ASSOCIATION OF INDEPENDENT SCHOOLS
4 Liberty Square
Boston, MA 02109

NATIONAL ASSOCIATION OF SECONDARY SCHOOL PRINCIPALS
1904 Association Drive
Reston, VA 22091

NATIONAL CONGRESS OF PARENTS AND TEACHERS
700 North Rush Street
Chicago, IL 60611

NATIONAL COUNCIL OF ADMINISTRATIVE WOMEN IN EDUCATION
1201 16th Street, N.W.
Washington, DC 20036

NATIONAL EDUCATION ASSOCIATION
1201 16th Street, N.W.
Washington, DC 20036

NATIONAL SCHOOL BOARDS ASSOCIATION
1055 Thomas Jefferson Street, N.W.
Suite 600
Washington, DC 20007

NATIONAL SCHOOL PUBLIC RELATIONS ASSOCIATION
1801 North Moore Street
Arlington, VA 22209

PHI DELTA KAPPA
Eighth and Union
P.O. Box 789
Bloomington, IN 47401

UNIVERSITY COUNCIL FOR EDUCATIONAL ADMINISTRATION
29 West Woodruff Avenue
Room 066
Columbus, OH 43210

Appendix III

DIRECTORY OF
STATE SCHOOL BOARD ASSOCIATIONS

ALABAMA ASSOCIATION OF SCHOOL BOARDS
Post Office Box 11475
Montgomery, AL 36111

ASSOCIATION OF ALASKA SCHOOL BOARDS
326 Fourth Street, Suite 204
Juneau, AK 99801

ARIZONA SCHOOL BOARDS ASSOCIATION
2602 West Osborn Road
Phoenix, AZ 85017

ARKANSAS SCHOOL BOARDS ASSOCIATION
815 Bishop Street
Little Rock, AR 72202

CALIFORNIA SCHOOL BOARDS ASSOCIATION
916 23rd Street
Sacramento, CA 95816

CONNECTICUT ASSOCIATION OF BOARDS OF EDUCATION, INC.
275 Windsor Street
Hartford, CT 06120

COLORADO ASSOCIATION OF SCHOOL BOARDS
1330 Logan Street
Denver, CO 80203

DELAWARE SCHOOL BOARDS ASSOCIATION
Bank of Delaware Bldg., Suite 204
P.O. Box 1277
Dover, DE 19901

BOARD OF EDUCATION OF THE DISTRICT OF COLUMBIA
415 Twelfth Street, N.W.
Washington, DC 20004

Information furnished by the National School Boards Association.

FLORIDA SCHOOL BOARDS ASSOCIATION, INC.
203 South Monroe Street
Tallahassee, FL 32301

GEORGIA SCHOOL BOARDS ASSOCIATION
3050 Presidential Drive, Suite 111
Atlanta, GA 30340

HAWAII STATE BOARD OF EDUCATION
Post Office Box 2360
Honolulu, HI 96804

IDAHO SCHOOL BOARDS ASSOCIATION
Post Office Box 2577
Boise, ID 83701

ILLINOIS ASSOCIATION OF SCHOOL BOARDS
1209 South Fifth Street
Springfield, IL 62703

INDIANA SCHOOL BOARDS ASSOCIATION
222 North New Jersey
Indianapolis, IN 46204

IOWA ASSOCIATION OF SCHOOL BOARDS
707 Savings and Loan Building
6th Avenue at Mulberry
Des Moines, IA 50309

KANSAS ASSOCIATION OF SCHOOL BOARDS
5401 Southwest 7th Avenue
Topeka, KS 66606

KENTUCKY SCHOOL BOARDS ASSOCIATION
Post Office Box 559
Englewood Office Park
Frankfort, KY 40602

LOUISIANA SCHOOL BOARDS ASSOCIATION
Post Office Box 80459
Baton Rouge, LA 70898

MAINE SCHOOL BOARDS ASSOCIATION
2 Central Plaza
Sewell Street
Augusta, ME 04330

MARYLAND ASSOCIATION OF BOARDS OF EDUCATION
130 Holiday Court, Suite 105
Annapolis, MD 21401

MASSACHUSETTS ASSOCIATION OF SCHOOL COMMITTEES, INC.
73 Tremont Street, Room 1115
Boston, MA 02108

MICHIGAN ASSOCIATION OF SCHOOL BOARDS, INC.
421 West Kalamazoo
Lansing, MI 48933

MINNESOTA SCHOOL BOARDS ASSOCIATION
Post Office Box 119
St. Peter, MN 56082

MISSISSIPPI SCHOOL BOARDS ASSOCIATION
Post Office Box 203
Clinton, MS 39056

MISSOURI SCHOOL BOARDS ASSOCIATION
305 Noyes Hall
University of Missouri-Columbia
Columbia, MO 65211

MONTANA SCHOOL BOARDS ASSOCIATION
501 North Sanders
Helena, MT 59601

NEBRASKA STATE SCHOOL BOARDS ASSOCIATION
The Executive Bldg., Room 305
521 South Fourteenth Street
Lincoln, NE 68508

NEVADA STATE SCHOOL BOARDS ASSOCIATION
1100 Kietzke Lane, Room 212
Reno, NV 89502

NEW HAMPSHIRE SCHOOL BOARDS ASSOCIATION
University of New Hampshire
Morrill Hall
Durham, NH 03824

NEW JERSEY SCHOOL BOARDS ASSOCIATION
315 West State Street, Box 909
Trenton, NJ 08605

NEW MEXICO SCHOOL BOARDS ASSOCIATION
207 Shelby Street
Santa Fe, NM 87501

NEW YORK STATE SCHOOL BOARDS ASSOCIATION, INC.
119 Washington Avenue
Albany, NY 12210

NORTH CAROLINA SCHOOL BOARDS ASSOCIATION, INC.
P. O. Box 2476
Raleigh, NC 27602

NORTH DAKOTA SCHOOL BOARDS ASSOCIATION
411 North Fourth Street
Bismarck, ND 58501

OHIO SCHOOL BOARDS ASSOCIATION
700 Brooksedge Blvd.
Westerville, OH 43081

OKLAHOMA STATE SCHOOL BOARDS ASSOCIATION, INC.
4001 North Lincoln, Suite 410
Oklahoma City, OK 73105

OREGON SCHOOL BOARDS ASSOCIATION
Post Office Box 1068
Salem, OR 97308

PENNSYLVANIA SCHOOL BOARDS ASSOCIATION, INC.
412 North Second Street
Harrisburg, PA 17101

RHODE ISLAND ASSOCIATION OF SCHOOL COMMITTEES
177 Airport Road
Warwick, RI 02889

SOUTH CAROLINA SCHOOL BOARDS ASSOCIATION
1706 Senate Street
Columbia, SC 29201

ASSOCIATED SCHOOL BOARDS OF SOUTH DAKOTA
P.O. Box 1211
Pierre, SD 57501

TENNESSEE SCHOOL BOARDS ASSOCIATION
323 McLemore Street, Ste. K
Nashville, TN 37203

TEXAS ASSOCIATION OF SCHOOL BOARDS
P. O. Box 400
Austin, TX 78767

UTAH SCHOOL BOARDS ASSOCIATION, INC.
199 East 7200 South
Midvale, UT 84047

VERMONT SCHOOL BOARDS ASSOCIATION, INC.
Box 339
Montpelier, VT 05602

VIRGIN ISLANDS BOARD OF EDUCATION
Commandant Gade O.V. No. 11
P.O. Box 9128
Charlotte Amalie
St. Thomas, VI 00801

VIRGINIA SCHOOL BOARDS ASSOCIATION
University of Virginia
Ruffner Hall
Charlottesville, VA 22903

Appendix III

WASHINGTON STATE SCHOOL DIRECTORS' ASSOCIATION
200 East Union Avenue
Olympia, WA 98501

WEST VIRGINIA SCHOOL BOARDS ASSOCIATION
P.O. Box 1008
Charleston, WV 25324

WISCONSIN ASSOCIATION OF SCHOOL BOARDS, INC.
122 W. Washington Avenue, Room 700
Madison, WI 53703

WYOMING SCHOOL BOARDS ASSOCIATION
P.O. Box 3274, University Station
University of Wyoming
Laramie, WY 82071

Appendix IV

STATE OFFICES OF THE NATIONAL PTA

ALABAMA CONGRESS OF PARENTS AND TEACHERS, INC.
207 North Jackson
Montgomery, AL 36104

ALASKA CONGRESS OF PARENTS AND TEACHERS
P.O. Box 680
Anchorage, AK 99510

ARIZONA CONGRESS OF PARENTS AND TEACHERS, INC.
2721 North Seventh Avenue
Phoenix, AZ 85007

ARKANSAS CONGRESS OF PARENTS AND TEACHERS, INC.
1201 McAlmont–P.O. Box 3017
Little Rock, AR 72203

CALIFORNIA CONGRESS OF PARENTS, TEACHERS, AND STUDENTS, INC.
930 Georgia Street
Los Angeles, CA 90015

COLORADO CONGRESS OF PARENTS, TEACHERS, AND STUDENTS
1005 Wadsworth Boulevard
Lakewood, CO 80215

THE PARENT-TEACHER ASSOCIATION OF CONNECTICUT, INC.
621 Burnside Avenue
East Hartford, CT 06108

DELAWARE CONGRESS OF PARENTS AND TEACHERS
92 South Gerald Drive
Newark, DE 19713

Information furnished by the National PTA.

D.C. CONGRESS OF PARENTS AND TEACHERS
J. O. Wilson Elementary School
660 K Street, N.E.
Washington, DC 20002

EUROPEAN CONGRESS OF AMERICAN PARENTS, TEACHERS,
AND STUDENTS
c/o Heidelberg American High School
APO New York 09102
Heidelberg MIL (2121) 8000

FLORIDA CONGRESS OF PARENTS AND TEACHERS, INC.
1741 Orlando Central Parkway
Orlando, FL 32809

GEORGIA CONGRESS OF PARENTS AND TEACHERS, INC.
114 Baker Street, N.E.
Atlanta, GA 30308

HAWAII CONGRESS OF PARENTS, TEACHERS, AND STUDENTS
677 Ala Moana Boulevard
Gold Bond Building, Suite 411
Honolulu, HI 96813

IDAHO CONGRESS OF PARENTS AND TEACHERS, INC.
620 North Sixth Street
Boise, ID 83702

ILLINOIS CONGRESS OF PARENTS AND TEACHERS
901 South Spring Street
Springfield, IL 62704

INDIANA CONGRESS OF PARENTS AND TEACHERS, INC.
2150 Lafayette Road
Indianapolis, IN 46222

IOWA CONGRESS OF PARENTS AND TEACHERS, INC.
412 Shops Building
Des Moines, IA 50309

KANSAS CONGRESS OF PARENTS AND TEACHERS
404 West Seventh Street
Topeka, KA 66603

KENTUCKY CONGRESS OF PARENTS AND TEACHERS
66 Fountain Place
Frankfort, KY 40601

LOUISIANA PARENT-TEACHER ASSOCIATION
Room 114, Laboratory School L.S.U.
P.O. Box 21550-A, University Station
Baton Rouge, LA 70893-5515

MAINE CONGRESS OF PARENTS AND TEACHERS, INC.
Route 1, Bigelow Road
East Lebanon, ME 04027

MARYLAND CONGRESS OF PARENTS AND TEACHERS, INC.
17 Commerce Street, Suite 100–102
Baltimore, MD 21202

MASSACHUSETTS PARENT-TEACHER-STUDENT ASSOCIATION
11 Muzzey Street
Lexington, MA 02173

MICHIGAN CONGRESS OF PARENTS, TEACHERS AND STUDENTS
1011 North Washington Avenue
Lansing, MI 48906

MINNESOTA CONGRESS OF PARENTS, TEACHERS AND STUDENTS
1910 West County Road B, Suite 102
Roseville, MN 55113-5494

MISSISSIPPI CONGRESS OF PARENTS AND TEACHERS
401 Unifirst Building
P.O. Box 1946 (use only for letters)
525 East Capital Street
Jackson, MS 39205

MISSOURI CONGRESS OF PARENTS AND TEACHERS
2101 Burlington Street
Columbia, MO 65202

MONTANA CONGRESS OF PARENTS AND TEACHERS, INC.
R.R. 4392
Great Falls, MT 59401

NEBRASKA CONGRESS OF PARENTS AND TEACHERS, INC.
2601 North 47th Street
Lincoln, NE 68504

NEVADA PARENT-TEACHER ASSOCIATION
P.O. Box 42996
Las Vegas, NV 89116-0996

NEW HAMPSHIRE CONGRESS OF PARENTS AND TEACHERS
R.R. 1, Box 442-Danville Road
Fremont, NH 03044

NEW JERSEY CONGRESS OF PARENTS AND TEACHERS
P.O. Box 1774, 900 Berkeley Avenue
Trenton, NJ 08607

NEW MEXICO CONGRESS OF PARENTS AND TEACHERS
118 Woodland Avenue, N.W.
Albuquerque, NM 87107

NEW YORK STATE CONGRESS OF PARENTS AND TEACHERS, INC.
119 Washington Avenue
Albany, NY 12210

NORTH CAROLINA CONGRESS OF PARENTS AND TEACHERS
P. O. Box 10607
Raleigh, NC 27605

NORTH DAKOTA CONGRESS OF PARENTS AND TEACHERS
810 Divide Avenue
Bismarck, ND 58501

OHIO CONGRESS OF PARENTS AND TEACHERS, INC.
427 East Town Street
Columbus, OH 43215

OKLAHOMA CONGRESS OF PARENTS AND TEACHERS, INC.
555 East Constitution Street
Norman, OK 73037

OREGON CONGRESS OF PARENTS AND TEACHERS, INC.
8050 S.E. 13th Avenue
Portland, OR 97202

PENNSYLVANIA CONGRESS OF PARENTS AND TEACHERS, INC.
P.O. Box 4384
4804 Derry Street
Harrisburg, PA 17111

RHODE ISLAND CONGRESS OF PARENTS AND TEACHERS
2020 Elmwood Avenue (Rear)
Warwick, RI 02888

SOUTH CAROLINA CONGRESS OF PARENTS AND TEACHERS
1826 Henderson Street
Columbia, SC 29201

SOUTH DAKOTA CONGRESS OF PARENTS AND TEACHERS
317 Iowa, S.E., Box 654
Huron, SD 57350

TENNESSEE CONGRESS OF PARENTS AND TEACHERS, INC.
1905 Acklen Avenue
Nashville, TN 37212

TEXAS CONGRESS OF PARENTS AND TEACHERS
408 West 11th Street
Austin, TX 78701

UTAH CONGRESS OF PARENTS AND TEACHERS
1037 East South Temple
Salt Lake City, UT 84102

VERMONT CONGRESS OF PARENTS AND TEACHERS
138 Main Street
Montpelier, VT 05602

VIRGINIA CONGRESS OF PARENTS AND TEACHERS
3810 Augusta Avenue
Richmond, VA 23230

WASHINGTON CONGRESS OF PARENTS, TEACHERS, AND STUDENTS, INC.
240 St. Helens Avenue
Tacoma, WA 98402

WEST VIRGINIA CONGRESS OF PARENTS AND TEACHERS, INC.
First Huntington Building
Room 1018, 421 Tenth Street
Huntington, WV 25701

WISCONSIN CONGRESS OF PARENTS AND TEACHERS, INC.
223 North Baldwin Street
Madison, WI 53703

WYOMING CONGRESS OF PARENTS AND TEACHERS
1115 Garfield
Laramie, WY 82070

—————————————————————— Appendix V
STATE DEPARTMENTS OF EDUCATION

State Department of Education	Mailing Address of Chief State School Officer
Alabama	State Office Building 501 Dexter Avenue Montgomery, AL 36130
Alaska	State Office Building Pouch F Juneau, AK 99811
American Samoa	Education Building Pago Pago, American Samoa 96799
Arizona	1535 West Jefferson Phoenix, AZ 85007
Arkansas	State Capitol Grounds Little Rock, AR 72201
California	721 Capitol Mall Sacramento, CA 95814
Colorado	State Office Building 201 E. Colfax Denver, CO 80203
Connecticut	P.O. Box 2219 Hartford, CT 06115
Delaware	Townsend Building P.O. Box 1402 Dover, DE 19901
District of Columbia	415 12th Street, N.W. Washington, DC 20004

SOURCE: Joanell Porter, *Education Directory: State Education Agency Officials 1981*, National Center for Education Statistics.

State Department of Education	Mailing Address of Chief State School Officer
Florida	Knott Building Tallahassee, FL 32301
Georgia	State Office Building Atlanta, GA 30334
Guam	P.O. Box "D.E." Agana, Guam 96910
Hawaii	1390 Miller Street Honolulu, HI 96813
Idaho	Len B. Jordan Office Building Boise, ID 83720
Illinois	100 North First Street Springfield, IL 62777
Indiana	Room 227, State House Indianapolis, IN 46204
Iowa	Grimes State Office Building Des Moines, IA 50319
Kansas	120 East 10th Street Topeka, KS 66612
Kentucky	State Department of Education Frankfort, KY 40601
Louisiana	626 North Fourth Street P.O. Box 44064 Baton Rouge, LA 70804
Maine	Education Building Augusta, ME 04333
Maryland	200 W. Baltimore Street Baltimore, MD 21201
Massachusetts	31 St. James Avenue Boston, MA 02116
Michigan	P.O. Box 30008 Lansing, MI 48909
Minnesota	Capitol Square Building St. Paul, MN 55101
Mississippi	Sillers State Office Building P.O. Box 771 Jackson, MS 39205
Missouri	Jefferson State Office Building P.O. Box 480, 100 E. Capitol Jefferson City, MO 65102
Montana	State Capitol, Room 106 Helena, MT 59620

State Department of Education	Mailing Address of Chief State School Officer
Nebraska	P.O. Box 94987 Lincoln, NE 68509
Nevada	Capitol Complex 400 West King Street Carson City, NV 89710
New Hampshire	State House Annex Concord, NH 03301
New Jersey	225 West State Street Trenton, NJ 08625
New Mexico	State Education Bldg. Santa Fe, NM 87501
New York	Education Building Albany, NY 12234
North Carolina	Education Building Raleigh, NC 27611
North Dakota	State Capitol Bismarck, ND 58505
Ohio	65 S. Front Street Columbus, OH 43215
Oklahoma	Oliver Hodge Memorial Education Building Oklahoma City, OK 73105
Oregon	700 Pringle Parkway SE Salem, OR 97310
Pennsylvania	Department of Education Box 911 Harrisburg, PA 17108
Puerto Rico	Education Building Hato Rey, PR 00900
Rhode Island	199 Promenade Street Providence, RI 02908
South Carolina	Rutledge Building 1429 Senate Street Columbia, SC 29201
South Dakota	Kneip Office Building Pierre, SD 57501
Tennessee	100 Cordell Hull Building Nashville, TN 37219
Texas	201 East 11th Street Austin, TX 78701

State Department of Education	Mailing Address of Chief State School Officer
Utah	250 East 5th South Salt Lake City, UT 84111
Vermont	State Department of Education Montpelier, VT 05602
Virginia	Box 6Q Richmond, VA 23216
Virgin Islands	P.O. Box 630 St. Thomas, VI 00802
Washington	Old Capitol Building FG–11 Olympia, WA 98504
West Virginia	1900 Washington Street, East Charleston, WV 25305
Wisconsin	125 South Webster Street Madison, WI 53707
Wyoming	Hathaway Building Cheyenne, WY 82002

Appendix VI
REGIONAL ACCREDITING ASSOCIATIONS

Association	State/Possession Served	Address
Middle States Association of Colleges and Schools	Delaware, District of Columbia, Maryland, New Jersey, New York, Pennsylvania, Puerto Rico, Virgin Islands	3624 Market St. Philadelphia, PA 19104
New England Association of Schools and Colleges	Connecticut, Maine, Massachusetts, New Hampshire, Rhode Island, Vermont	131 Middlesex Tpke. Burlington, MA 01803
North Central Association of Colleges and Schools	Arizona, Arkansas, Colorado, Illinois, Indiana, Iowa, Kansas, Michigan, Minnesota, Missouri, Nebraska, New Mexico, North Dakota, Ohio, Oklahoma, South Dakota, West Virginia, Wisconsin, Wyoming	P.O. Box 18 Boulder, CO 80306
Northwest Association of Schools and Colleges	Alaska, Idaho, Montana, Nevada, Oregon, Utah, Washington	3700-B University Way, N.E. Seattle, WA 98105
Southern Association of Colleges and Schools	Alabama, Florida, Georgia, Kentucky, Louisiana, Mississippi, North Carolina, South Carolina, Tennessee, Texas, Virginia	795 Peachtree St. NE Atlanta, GA 30308
Western Association of Schools and Colleges	American Samoa, California, Guam, Hawaii, Trust Territory of the Pacific	1614 Rollins Rd. Burlingame, CA 94010

Appendix VII
ERIC CLEARINGHOUSES

ADULT, CAREER, AND VOCATIONAL EDUCATION
Ohio State University
Center for Vocational Education
1960 Kenny Road
Columbus, OH 43210

COUNSELING AND PERSONNEL SERVICES
University of Michigan
2108 School of Education Building
Ann Arbor, MI 48109

EDUCATIONAL MANAGEMENT
University of Oregon
Eugene, OR 97403

ELEMENTARY AND EARLY CHILDHOOD EDUCATION
University of Illinois
College of Education
Urbana, IL 61801

HANDICAPPED AND GIFTED CHILDREN
Council for Exceptional Children
1920 Association Drive
Reston, VA 22091

HIGHER EDUCATION
George Washington University
One Dupont Circle, N.W., Suite 630
Washington, DC 20036

INFORMATION RESOURCES
Syracuse University
School of Education
130 Huntington Hall
Syracuse, NY 13210

JUNIOR COLLEGES
University of California at Los Angeles
96 Powell Library Building
Los Angeles, CA 90024

LANGUAGES AND LINGUISTICS
Center for Applied Linguistics
3520 Prospect Street, N.W.
Washington, DC 20007

READING AND COMMUNICATION SKILLS
National Council of Teachers of English
1111 Kenyon Road
Urbana, IL 61801

RURAL EDUCATION AND SMALL SCHOOLS
New Mexico State University
Box 3AP
Las Cruces, NM 88003

SCIENCE, MATHEMATICS, AND ENVIRONMENTAL EDUCATION
Ohio State University
1200 Chambers Road, 3rd Floor
Columbus, OH 43212

SOCIAL STUDIES/SOCIAL SCIENCE EDUCATION
Social Science Education Consortium, Inc.
855 Broadway
Boulder, CO 80302

TEACHER EDUCATION
American Association of Colleges for Teacher Education
One Dupont Circle, N.W., Suite 610
Washington, DC 20036

TESTS, MEASUREMENT, AND EVALUATION
Educational Testing Service
Rosedale Road
Princeton, NJ 08541

URBAN EDUCATION
Teachers College, Columbia University
Box 40
525 West 120th Street
New York, NY 10027

─────────────────────────────── Appendix VIII
PERIODICALS OF GENERAL INTEREST TO EDUCATIONAL ADMINISTRATORS

ADMINISTRATIVE SCIENCE QUARTERLY
Malott Hall
Cornell University
Ithaca, NY 14853

ADMINISTRATOR'S NOTEBOOK
Midwest Administration Center
University of Chicago
5835 S. Kimbark Avenue
Chicago, IL 60637

AMERICAN EDUCATIONAL RESEARCH JOURNAL
American Educational Research Association
1230 17th Street, N.W.
Washington, DC 20036

AMERICAN JOURNAL OF EDUCATION
University of Chicago Press
5801 S. Ellis Avenue
Chicago, IL 60637

AMERICAN SCHOOL BOARD JOURNAL
1055 Thomas Jefferson Street, N.W.
Washington, DC 20007

CANADIAN ADMINISTRATOR
Department of Educational Administration
University of Alberta
Edmonton, AB T6G 2G5
CANADA

EXECUTIVE EDUCATOR
National School Boards Association
1055 Thomas Jefferson Street, N.W.
Washington, DC 20007

CLEARING HOUSE
Heldref Publications
4000 Albemarle Street, N.W.
Washington, DC 20016

EDUCATION CANADA
Canadian Education Association
252 Bloor Street, W., Suite S 850
Toronto, ON M5S 1V5
CANADA

EDUCATIONAL ADMINISTRATION ABSTRACTS
Sage Publications, Inc.
275 South Beverly Drive
Beverly Hills, CA 90212

EDUCATIONAL ADMINISTRATION QUARTERLY
Sage Publications, Inc.
275 South Beverly Drive
Beverly Hills, CA 90212

EDUCATIONAL FORUM
Kappa Delta Pi
P.O. Box A
West Lafayette, IN 47906

EDUCATIONAL LEADERSHIP
Association for Supervision and Curriculum Development
225 N. Washington Street
Alexandria, VA 22314

EDUCATIONAL RESEARCHER
American Educational Research Association
1230 17th Street, N.W.
Washington, DC 20036

HARVARD EDUCATIONAL REVIEW
Business Office
Longfellow Hall
13 Appian Way
Cambridge, MA 02138

JOURNAL OF EDUCATIONAL ADMINISTRATION
University of New England
Armidale, New South Wales 2351
AUSTRALIA

JOURNAL OF EDUCATIONAL ADMINISTRATION AND HISTORY
School of Education
The University of Leeds
LS2 9JT ENGLAND

JOURNAL OF EDUCATIONAL EQUITY AND LEADERSHIP
Sage Publications
275 South Beverly Drive
Beverly Hills, CA 90212

JOURNAL OF EDUCATIONAL RESEARCH
Heldref Publications
4000 Albemarle Street, N.W., Suite 504
Washington, DC 20016

JOURNAL OF LAW AND EDUCATION
Jefferson Law Book Co.
P.O. Box 1936
Cincinnati, OH 45201

NASSP BULLETIN
National Association of Secondary School Principals
1904 Association Drive
Reston, VA 22091

NOLPE SCHOOL LAW JOURNAL
5401 S.W. 7th Avenue
Topeka, KS 66606

PERSONNEL ADMINISTRATOR
American Society for Personnel Administration
30 Park Drive
Berea, OH 44017

PHI DELTA KAPPAN
8th and Union
P.O. Box 789
Bloomington, IN 47402

PRINCIPAL
National Association of Elementary School Principals
1801 N. Moore Street
Arlington, VA 22209

REVIEW OF EDUCATIONAL RESEARCH
American Educational Research Association
1230 17th Street, N.W.
Washington, DC 20036

SCHOOL BUSINESS AFFAIRS
Association of School Business Officials of the
United States and Canada
720 Garden Street
Park Ridge, IL 60068

TEACHERS COLLEGE RECORD
Teachers College
Columbia University
525 W. 120th Street
New York, NY 10027

TODAY'S EDUCATION
National Education Association
1201 Sixteenth Street, N.W.
Washington, DC 20036

Appendix IX

JOURNALS REVIEWED FOR ABSTRACTING BY *EDUCATIONAL ADMINISTRATION ABSTRACTS*

Academe
Administration in Mental Health
Administrative Science Quarterly
Administrator's Bulletin
Administrator's Notebook
Adult Education
AEDS Journal
Alberta Journal of Educational Research
Alternative Futures
American Annals of the Deaf
American Educational Research Journal
American Journal of Education
American Journal of Mental Deficiency
American Journal of Sociology
American School Board Journal
American Sociological Review
Australian Journal of Adult Education
Australian Journal of Education
B. C. Journal of Special Education
Behavioral Science
British Journal of Educational Studies
British Journal of Educational Technology
Business Horizons
California Management Review
Cambridge Journal of Education
Canadian Administrator
Canadian and International Education
Canadian Journal of Education
Canadian Journal of Higher Education
Canadian Public Administration
Canadian Review of Sociology and Anthropology
Catalyst for Change
CEFP Journal
Centre for Educational Policy and Management Bulletin
Change
Clearing House
College and University
Community College Frontiers
Community College Review
Community Education Journal
Community and Junior College Journal
Daedalus

SOURCE: *Educational Administration Abstracts*, a publication of The University Council for Eductional Administration (in cooperation with Texas A and M University), Spring 1982. Reprinted with permission.

Education
Education Canada
Education for Development
Education and Training of the Mentally Retarded
Education and Urban Society
Educational Administration
Educational Administration Quarterly
Educational Considerations
Educational Forum
Educational Leadership
Educational Philosophy and Theory
Educational Record
Educational Researcher
Educational Technology
Elementary School Journal
Evaluation Newsletter
Exceptional Children
Futures
Futurist
Harvard Educational Review
High School Journal
Higher Education
Human Organization
Human Relations
Human Resource Management
Indian Educational Review
Industrial and Labor Relations Review
Inequality in Education
Integrateducation
Interchange
Journal of American Planning Association
Journal of Applied Behavioral Science
Journal of Applied Psychology
Journal of Applied Rehabilitation Counseling
Journal of Church and State
Journal of Collective Negotiations in the Public Sector
Journal of College and University Personnel Association
Journal of Conflict Resolution
Journal of Curriculum Studies
Journal of Education
Journal of Education Finance
Journal of Educational Administration
Journal of Educational Administration and History
Journal of Educational Communication
Journal of Educational Psychology
Journal of Educational Research
Journal of Educational Thought
Journal of Experimental Education
Journal of Higher Education
Journal of Human Resources
Journal of Law and Education
Journal of Learning Disabilities
Journal of Management Studies
Journal of the National Association for Women Deans, Administrators, and Counselors
Journal of Negro Education
Journal of Personality and Social Psychology
Journal of Research and Development in Education
Journal of Social Issues
Journal of Special Education
Journal of Speech and Hearing Disorders
Journal of Teacher Education
Kappa Delta Pi Record
Management Science
Manitoba Journal of Education
Mental Retardation
NASSP Bulletin
New York University Education Quarterly
NOLPE School Law Journal
Personnel
Personnel Administrator
Personnel and Guidance Journal
Personnel Journal
Personnel Psychology
Phi Delta Kappan
Planning and Changing
Planning for Higher Education
Policy Sciences
Policy Studies Journal
Policy Studies Review

Principal
Psychological Bulletin
Public Administration Review
Public Personnel Management
Research in Higher Education
Review of Educational Research
Simulation and Games
Sloan Management Review
Social Forces
Social Psychology Quarterly
Social Science Quarterly
Society
Socio-Economic Planning Sciences
Sociological Inquiry
Sociology of Education
Teachers College Record
Technological Forecasting and Social Change
THE Journal
Theory into Practice
University Administration
Urban Affairs Quarterly
Urban Education
Urban Review
USA Today

———————————————————— Appendix X
UNIVERSITY COUNCIL FOR EDUCATIONAL ADMINISTRATION: MEMBER UNIVERSITIES

University of Alberta
Arizona State University
University of Arkansas
Boston University
University of British Columbia
University of Cincinnati
University of Connecticut
University of Florida
Fordham University
Georgia State University
University of Houston
University of Illinois
Illinois State University
Northern Illinois University
Indiana University
University of Iowa
University of Kansas
University of Kentucky
University of Maryland
University of Minnesota
University of Missouri
University of Nebraska-Lincoln
New York University

State University of NY/Buffalo
Ohio State University
University of Oklahoma
Oklahoma State University
University of Oregon
Pennsylvania State University
University of Pittsburgh
University of Rochester
Rutgers University
St. John's University
Temple University
University of Tennessee
Texas A and M University
University of Texas at Austin
University of Toledo
University of Tulsa
University of Utah
University of Virginia
Washington State University
Wayne State University
University of Wisconsin-Madison
University of Wisconsin-Milwaukee

SOURCE: University Council for Educational Administration, *University Membership Mailing List, 1982–83*. Reprinted with permission.

Appendix XI

UNIVERSITY COUNCIL FOR EDUCATIONAL ADMINISTRATION: PARTNERSHIP SCHOOL DISTRICTS

Austin Independent School District, TX
Columbus Public Schools, OH
Detroit Public Schools, MI
East Brunswick Public Schools, NJ
East Syracuse—Minoa School District, NY
Edmonton Public School District, Alberta, CANADA
Fairfax County Public Schools, VA
Huntington Union Free School District, NY
Jefferson County Public Schools, CO
Lincoln Public Schools, NE
Little Rock School District, AR
Mesa Unified School District No. 4, AZ
Milwaukee Public Schools, WI
Monroe County Community Schools, IN
Norfolk Public Schools, VA
Oklahoma City Public Schools, OK
Orange County Public Schools, FL
Seattle Public Schools, WA
Shawnee Mission Public Schools, KS
Tacoma Public Schools, WA
Tulsa Public Schools, OK
Wake County Public Schools, NC
Wausau School District, WI

SOURCE: University Council for Educational Administration (untitled and undated brochure). Reprinted with permission.

Appendix XII

U.S. DEPARTMENT OF EDUCATION: REGIONAL OFFICES

Information furnished by the U.S. Department of Education.

Region	States/Possessions Served	Address
1	Connecticut, Maine, Massachusetts, New Hampshire, Rhode Island, Vermont	John F. Kennedy Federal Office Bldg. McCormack PO & Ct. Hs. Room 542, MS 526 Boston, MA 02109
2	New Jersey, New York, Puerto Rico, Virgin Islands	26 Federal Plaza New York, NY 10278
3	Delaware, District of Columbia, Maryland, Pennsylvania, Virginia, West Virginia	3535 Market Street Philadelphia, PA 19101
4	Alabama, Florida, Georgia, Kentucky, Mississippi, North Carolina, South Carolina, Tennessee	101 Marietta Tower Atlanta, GA 30323
5	Illinois, Indiana, Michigan, Minnesota, Ohio, Wisconsin	16th Floor 300 South Wacker Drive Chicago, IL 60606
6	Arkansas, Louisiana, New Mexico, Oklahoma, Texas	1200 Main Tower Dallas, TX 75202
7	Iowa, Kansas, Missouri, Nebraska	324 East 11th Street Kansas City, MO 64106
8	Colorado, Montana, North Dakota, South Dakota, Utah, Wyoming	1961 Stout St. Denver, CO 80294
9	American Samoa, Arizona, California, Guam, Hawaii, Nevada, Trust Territory of the Pacific	Federal Office Building 50 United Nations Plaza San Francisco, CA 94102
10	Alaska, Idaho, Oregon, Washington	2901 Third Avenue Seattle, WA 98121

Appendix XIII

BUREAU OF INDIAN AFFAIRS: AREA OFFICES

Area	Headquarters	Serving
Aberdeen	115 Fourth Avenue, S.E. Aberdeen, SD 57401	Nebraska, North Dakota, South Dakota
Albuquerque	5301 Central Avenue, N.E. Albuquerque, NM 87108	Colorado and New Mexico
Anadarko	Federal Building P.O. Box 368 Anadarko, OK 73005	Kansas and West Oklahoma
Billings	316 North 26th Street Billings, MT 59101	Montana and Wyoming
Eastern	1951 Constitution Ave., N.W. Washington, D.C. 20245	New York, North Carolina, Louisiana, Mississippi, and Florida
Juneau	Federal Building Box 3-8000 Juneau, AK 99802	Alaska
Minneapolis	Chamber of Commerce Building 15 South 5th Street Minneapolis, MN 55402	Minnesota, Iowa, Michigan, and Wisconsin
Muskogee	Old Federal Building Muskogee, OK 74401	East Oklahoma
Navajo	Window Rock, AZ 86515	Arizona (Navajo Reservation only), Utah, and New Mexico
Phoenix	3030 N. Central P.O. Box 7007 Phoenix, AZ 85011	Arizona and Nevada

Portland	1425 N.E. Irving Street P.O. Box 3785 Portland, OR 97208	Oregon, Washington, and Idaho
Sacramento	Federal Office Building 2800 Cottage Way Sacramento, CA 95825	California

Appendix XIV

NCATE-ACCREDITED PROGRAMS: SCHOOL PRINCIPALSHIPS, SUPERVISION/CURRICULUM DEVELOPMENT, AND SCHOOL SUPERINTENDENCY, 1982–1983

SOURCE: *NCATE 29th Annual List of Accredited Programs, 1982–83.* Reprinted with permission.

Program*

State	Institution	Principalship	Supervisor	Superintendency
Alabama	Alabama A & M University	M	M	—
	Alabama State University	M	—	—
	Auburn University	MSD	MSD	SD
	Jacksonville State University	M	M	—
	Samford University	M	—	—
	Univ. of Alabama: Birmingham	MS	—	S
	Univ. of Alabama: University	M	M	—
	Univ. of South Alabama	(M) (S)	(M) (S)	(S)
Arizona	Arizona State Univ.	MSD	MSD	SD
	Northern Arizona University	MSD	SD	SD
	University of Arizona	SD	SD	SD
Arkansas	Arkansas State University	MS	MS	S
	Univ. of Arkansas: Fayetteville	MSD	MSD	SD
	Univ. of Central Arkansas	M	M	—
California	California State Univ.: Chico	M	M	—
	California State Univ.: Fresno	M	M	—

*Symbols used:
M = master's degree program
S = specialist degree program
D = doctoral degree program
(M) = post-baccalaureate but nondegree program
(S) = post-master's but nondegree program

	California State Univ.: Fullerton	M	—
	California State Univ.: Hayward	M	—
	California State Univ.: Los Angeles	M	—
	California State Univ.: Sacramento	M	—
	College of Notre Dame	M	—
	San Diego State Univ.	M	M(S)
	San Francisco State Univ.	M	(S)
	San Jose State Univ.	M	—
	Univ. of the Pacific	MD	D
	Univ. of Southern California	MSD	SD
Colorado	Colorado State Univ.	M	M
	Univ. of Colorado System (Boulder, Colorado Springs, Denver)	MSD	MSD
	Univ. of Denver	MD	MD
	Univ. of North. Colorado	MS	MD
	Western State College	M	—
Connecticut	Univ. of Connecticut	SD	SD
	Univ. of Hartford	M	M
Dist. of Columbia	George Washington Univ.	M	M
Florida	Florida A & M Univ.	M	—
	Florida Atlantic Univ.	MSD	MSD
	Florida State Univ.	MSD	MSD
	Univ. of Florida	MSD	MSD
	Univ. of Miami	MSD	MSD
Georgia	Atlanta Univ.	MS	S

235

State	Institution	Principalship	Supervisor	Superintendency
	Georgia Southern College	MS	MS	S
	Georgia State Univ.	MSD	MSD	S
	Univ. of Georgia	MSD	MSD	SD
	Valdosta State College	MS	MS	S
	West Georgia College	MS	MS	–
Idaho	Univ. of Idaho	MSD	M	SD
Illinois	Bradley Univ.	M	–	–
	Concordia Teachers College	M	M	–
	DePaul Univ.	M	M	–
	Eastern Illinois Univ.	M	–	S
	Illinois State Univ.	MSD	–	SD
	Loyola Univ.	MD	MD	D
	Northern Illinois Univ.	MSD	MSD	SD
	Roosevelt Univ.	M	M	–
	Southern Illinois Univ.: Carbondale	MSD	MSD	SD
	Southern Illinois Univ.: Edwardsville	MS	–	S
	Univ. of Illinois	MSD	MSD	SD
	Western Illinois Univ.	S	S	S
Indiana	Ball State Univ.	MSD	MSD	SD
	Indiana State Univ.: Terre Haute	MS	MS	SD
	Indiana Univ.: Bloomington	MSD	MSD	SD
	Univ. of Evansville	M	–	–

236

Iowa	Drake Univ.	MSD	MSD	SD
	Iowa State Univ.	M	M	SD
	Univ. of Iowa	MSD	MD	SD
	Univ. of Northern Iowa	MS	MS	S
Kansas	Emporia State Univ.	MS	MS	S
	Ft. Hays State Univ.	M	M	–
	Kansas State Univ.	MD	MD	D
	Pittsburg State Univ.	MS	–	S
	Univ. of Kansas	MSD	MSD	SD
	Washburn Univ.	M	–	–
	Wichita State Univ.	MS	MS	S
Kentucky	Eastern Kentucky Univ.	M	M	–
	Morehead State Univ.	M	M	–
	Murray State Univ.	M	M	S
	Univ. of Kentucky	MSD	MSD	SD
	Univ. of Louisville	MS	MS	S
	Western Kentucky Univ.	MS	M	S
Louisiana	Louisiana State Univ.: Baton Rouge	M	M	–
	McNeese State Univ.	MS	MS	S
	Nicholls State Univ.	M	M	–
	Northeast Louisiana Univ.	MS	MS	S
	Northwestern State Univ.	M	–	–
	Southeastern Louisiana Univ.	MS	M	S
	Univ. of New Orleans	MD	MD	D
	Univ. of Southwestern Louisiana	M	M	–

237

State	Institution	Principalship	Supervisor	Superintendency
Maine	Univ. of Maine: Orono	M	M	—
Maryland	Bowie State College	M	M	—
	Morgan State University	M	M	—
	Univ. of Maryland	MSD	MSD	SD
Massachusetts	Boston College	MSD	MSD	SD
	Boston Univ.	MSD	MSD	SD
	Harvard Univ.	MSD	MSD	SD
	Northeastern Univ.	M	—	S
	Salem State College	M	—	—
	Univ. of Lowell	M	M	—
	Univ. of Massachusetts	MSD	MSD	SD
	Worcester State College	M	M	—
Michigan	Andrews Univ.	M	—	—
	Central Michigan Univ.	MS	MS	S
	Eastern Michigan Univ.	MS	M	S
	Michigan State University	MSD	MSD	SD
	Northern Michigan Univ.	M	—	—
	Univ. of Michigan	MD	MD	D
	Wayne State Univ.	MSD	MSD	SD
	Western Michigan Univ.	MSD	MSD	SD
Minnesota	Bemidji State Univ.	M	—	—
	College of St. Thomas	MS	M	S

	Mankato State Univ.	MS	S
	St. Cloud State Univ.	MS	S
	Univ. of Minnesota: Minneapolis	MSD	SD
	Winona State Univ.	MS	S
Mississippi	Delta State Univ.	M	S
	Jackson State Univ.	MS	S
	Mississippi College	M	—
	Mississippi State Univ.	MS	D
	Univ. of Mississippi	MSD	SD
	Univ. of Southern Mississippi	MS	SD
Missouri	Central Missouri State Univ.	MS	S
	Northeast Missouri State Univ.	MS	S
	Northwest Missouri State Univ.	M	—
	Southeast Missouri State Univ.	MS	S
	Southwest Missouri State Univ.	MS	S
	St. Louis Univ.	MSD	SD
	Univ. of Missouri: Columbia	MSD	SD
	Univ. of Missouri: Kansas City	MSD	SD
	Univ. of Missouri: St. Louis	MSD	(S)
	Washington Univ.	SD	—
Montana	Montana State Univ.	MD	D
	Univ. of Montana	MSD	SD
Nebraska	Chadron State College	MS	S
	Concordia Teachers College	M	—
	Creighton Univ.	M	—
	Kearney State College	M	S

239

Program*

State	Institution	Principalship	Supervisor	Superintendency
	Univ. of Nebraska: Lincoln	M(S)D	M(S)D	(S)D
	Univ. of Nebraska: Omaha	M	S	S
Nevada	Univ. of Nevada: Reno	M	M	—
New Hampshire	Plymouth State College	M	M	—
	Univ. of New Hampshire	M	—	S
New Jersey	Glassboro State College	M	M	—
	Jersey City State College	M	M	—
	Kean College	M	M	—
	Montclair State College	M	—	—
	Rider College	M	M	—
	Rutgers Univ.: New Brunswick	M	MD	SD
	Seton Hall Univ.	M	M	—
	Wm. Patterson College	M	—	—
New Mexico	Eastern New Mexico Univ.	MS	S	S
	New Mexico State Univ.	MSD	SD	SD
	Univ. of New Mexico	MSD	MSD	SD
New York	CUNY: City College	MS	MS	(S)
	CUNY: Hunter College	S	S	—
	Columbia Univ. Teachers College	MSD	MSD	SD
	Fordham Univ.	MSD	MSD	SD
	Hofstra Univ.	SD	MSD	SD

	New York Univ.	MSD	SD
	Syracuse Univ.	MSD	SD
North Carolina	Appalachian State Univ.	MS	S
	Duke Univ.	MSD	SD
	East Carolina Univ.	MS	S
	North Carolina A&T State Univ.	M	—
	North Carolina Central Univ.	M	—
	North Carolina State Univ.	M	—
	Univ. of North Carolina: Chapel Hill	MSD	SD
	Univ. of North Carolina: Greensboro	MD	SD
	Western Carolina Univ.	MS	S
North Dakota	Univ. of North Dakota	MSD	SD
Ohio	Bowling Green State Univ.	MSD	SD
	Cleveland State Univ.	M	—
	John Carroll Univ.	M	—
	Kent State Univ.	MSD	SD
	Miami Univ.	MSD	SD
	Ohio State Univ.	MSD	SD
	Ohio Univ.	MSD	SD
	Univ. of Akron	MD	SD
	Univ. of Cincinnati	MD	SD
	Univ. of Dayton	MSD	SD
	Univ. of Toledo	M	—
	Wright State Univ.	MSD	SD
	Youngstown State Univ.	M	S
Oklahoma	Central State Univ.	M	—
	Northeastern Oklahoma State Univ.	M	—

State	Institution	Principalship	Supervisor	Superintendency
	Oklahoma State Univ.	MD	MD	D
	Univ. of Oklahoma	MD	MD	D
	Univ. of Tulsa	M	–	D
Oregon	Portland State Univ.	S	–	–
	Univ. of Oregon	MD	MD	SD
Pennsylvania	California State College	–	M	–
	Cheyney State College	M	M	–
	Edinboro State College	MS	S	–
	Indiana Univ. of Pa.	–	M	–
	Lehigh Univ.	M	MD	SD
	Millersville State College	–	S	–
	Pennsylvania State Univ.	MD	MD	D
	Shippensburg State College	M	M	–
	Temple Univ.	M(S)D	M(S)D	(S)D
	Univ. of Pittsburgh	MSD	MSD	SD
	Univ. of Scranton	M	M	–
Puerto Rico	Univ. of Puerto Rico	M	–	–
Rhode Island	Rhode Island College	MS	–	–
South Carolina	Clemson Univ.	M	M	S
	The Citadel	M	–	–
	Univ. of South Carolina	MSD	MD	SD

South Dakota	Northern State College	M		–
	Univ. of South Dakota	MSD		SD
Tennessee	Austin Peay State Univ.	M	M	–
	East Tennessee State Univ.	MSD	MSD	SD
	Memphis State Univ.	MSD	MSD	SD
	Middle Tennessee State Univ.	MS	MS	S
	Tennessee State Univ.	MS	MS	S
	Tennessee Technological Univ.	MS	MS	S
	Univ. of Tennessee: Chattanooga	M	M	–
	Univ. of Tennessee: Knoxville	MSD	MSD	SD
	Univ. of Tennessee: Martin	M	M	–
	Vanderbilt Univ. (Peabody)	M	SD	SD
Texas	Baylor Univ.	M	M	(S)
	East Texas State Univ.	M	M	(S)
	Lamar Univ.	–	M	–
	Midwestern State Univ.	M	–	–
	North Texas State Univ.	MD	M	D
	Pan American Univ.	M	M	(S)
	Sam Houston State Univ.	M	M	S
	Southwest Texas State Univ.	M	M	(S)
	Stephen F. Austin State Univ.	–	–	–
	Tarleton State Univ.	M	M	S
	Texas A and I Univ.	M	–	(S)
	Texas A and M Univ.	MD	M	D
	Texas Christian Univ.	–	MD	–
	Texas Southern Univ.	MD	M	(S)D
	Texas Tech Univ.	MD	MD	SD
	Texas Woman's Univ.	–	MD	–

243

State	Institution	Principalship	Supervisor	Superintendency
	Trinity Univ.	M	M	S
	Univ. of Houston	MD	MD	D
	Univ. of Houston at Clear Lake City	M	M	–
	Univ. of Texas: Austin	MD	MD	D
	Univ. of Texas: El Paso	M	M	S
	West Texas State Univ.	M	–	–
Utah	Brigham Young Univ.	MSD	MSD	SD
	Univ. of Utah	SD	–	SD
	Utah State Univ.	–	MD	–
Vermont	Univ. of Vermont	MS	M	S
Virginia	College of William & Mary	MSD	M	SD
	George Mason Univ.	M	M	–
	James Madison Univ.	M	–	–
	Longwood College	M	M	–
	Old Dominion Univ.	MS	MS	–
	Radford Univ.	M	M	–
	Univ. of Virginia	MSD	MSD	SD
	Virginia Commonwealth	M	M	–
	Virginia Polytechnic Institute	MD	MD	D
Washington	Central Washington Univ.	M	–	–
	Eastern Washington Univ.	M	–	–
	Pacific Lutheran Univ.	M	–	–

	Seattle Univ.	M	M	—
	Univ. of Puget Sound	M	M	—
	Univ. of Washington	MD	MD	D
	Washington State Univ.	MD	MD	D
	Western Washington Univ.	M	M	—
West Virginia	Marshall Univ.	M	M	—
	W. Va. College of Graduate Studies Institute	M	—	S
	West Virginia Univ.	MD	MD	SD
Wisconsin	Univ. of Wisconsin: La Crosse	—	M	—
	Univ. of Wisconsin: Oshkosh	M	M	—
	Univ. of Wisconsin: River Falls	M	M	—
Wyoming	Univ. of Wyoming	MSD	MSD	SD

245

Appendix XV
KEY GOVERNMENTAL AND INTERGOVERNMENTAL OFFICES

BUREAU OF INDIAN AFFAIRS
U.S. Department of the Interior
"C" Street, N.W.
Washington, DC 20240

COMMISSION ON CIVIL RIGHTS
1121 Vermont Avenue, N.W.
Washington, DC 20425

DEPARTMENT OF DEFENSE DEPENDENTS SCHOOLS
Room 152
Hoffman Building
Alexandria, VA 22331

EDUCATION COMMISSION OF THE STATES
300 Lincoln Tower Building
1860 Lincoln Street
Denver, CO 80295

EQUAL EMPLOYMENT OPPORTUNITY COMMISSION
2401 "E" Street, N.W.
Washington, DC 20506

LIBRARY OF CONGRESS
10 First Street, S.E.
Washington, DC 20540

NATIONAL FOUNDATION OF THE ARTS AND THE HUMANITIES
2401 "E" Street, N.W.
Washington, DC 20506

NATIONAL SCHOOL LUNCH PROGRAM
U.S. Department of Agriculture
Fourteenth Street and Independence Avenue, S.W.
Washington, DC 20250

NATIONAL SCIENCE FOUNDATION
1800 "G" Street, N.W.
Washington, DC 20550

OFFICE OF OVERSEAS SCHOOLS
U.S. Department of State
2201 "C" Street, N.W.
Washington, DC 20520

PEACE CORPS
806 Connecticut Avenue, N.W.
Washington, DC 20226

UNITED NATIONS EDUCATIONAL, SCIENTIFIC AND
CULTURAL ORGANIZATION
Place de Fontenoy
Paris 75700, FRANCE

—or—

UN Liaison Office
2401 U.N. Building
New York, NY 10017

U.S. DEPARTMENT OF EDUCATION
400 Maryland Avenue, S.W.
Washington, DC 20202

VISTA (Volunteers in Service to America)
806 Connecticut Avenue, N.W.
Washington, DC 20525

About the Author

EDWARD L. DEJNOZKA is Professor of Educational Administration at Florida Atlantic University in Boca Raton and former dean, College of Education, University of Nebraska at Omaha. He is the senior author of the *American Educators' Encyclopedia* (Greenwood Press, 1982), selected by *Choice* as an Outstanding Academic Book for 1982 and chosen by the Reference Sources Committee of the American Library Association as an Outstanding Reference Book for 1982. Dejnozka has also published articles in *School Executive, Journal of Educational Sociology, Elementary School Journal,* and the *Peabody Journal of Education,* among many others.